101 $ Things Everyone Should Know about

ECONOMICS

2ND EDITION

From Securities and Derivatives to Interest Rates
and Hedge Funds, the Basics of Economics and
What They Mean for You

Peter Sander, MBA

Aadamsmedia

AVON, MASSACHUSETTS

Published by
Adams Media, a division of F+W Media, Inc.
57 Littlefield Street, Avon, MA 02322 U.S.A.
www.adamsmedia.com

ISBN 10: 1-4405-7271-2
ISBN 13: 978-1-4405-7271-5
eISBN 10: 1-4405-7272-0
eISBN 13: 978-1-4405-7272-2

Printed in the United States of America.

10 9 8 7 6 5 4 3 2 1

Library of Congress Cataloging-in-Publication Data
Sander, Peter J.
  101 things everyone should know about economics / Peter Sander. -- 2nd Edition.
     pages cm
  Includes bibliographical references and index.
  ISBN-13: 978-1-4405-7271-5 (pb : alk. paper)
  ISBN-10: 1-4405-7271-2 (pb : alk. paper)
  ISBN-13: 978-1-4405-7272-2 (eISBN)
  ISBN-10: 1-4405-7272-0 (eISBN)
1. Economics. 2. Finance, Personal. I. Title. II. Title: One hundred one things everyone should
know about economics. III. Title: A hundred one things everyone should know about economics.
  HB171.5.S2586 2014
  330--dc23

                                    2013034560

This book is available at quantity discounts for bulk purchases.
For information, please call 1-800-289-0963.

DEDICATION

101 Things Everyone Should Know about Economics, 2nd Edition is dedicated to you who are in charge of your finances today—or will be someday—who strive to make sense of the complex economic world around you. You want to understand how it all affects you, your family, and your future; you seek what you should know and why you should know it. This edition in particular is dedicated to making sense of the dismal years of the Great Recession, to learning its lessons, and to doing well for yourself and your family regardless of the current economic climate.

ACKNOWLEDGMENTS

I would like to recognize my editor, Peter Archer, for coming up with the "101 Economics" concept as a simplified, common-sense way to present a difficult and typically dry topic. Of course, as with all of my books, my boys Julian and Jonathan and new life partner Marjorie get credit for the inspiration and support to keep writing.

Contents

CHAPTER 3:

Money, Prices, and Interest Rates . . . 59

CHAPTER 4:

Banks and Central Banking . . . 81

CHAPTER 5:

Government and Government Programs . . . 107

CHAPTER 6:

Economic Schools and Tools . . . 143

CHAPTER 7:

Finance and Financial Markets . . . 169

CHAPTER 8:
Trade and International Economics . . . 225

Introduction

What is the world coming to?

You read the headlines. Two appeared recently on the front page of the same newspaper (for those of you who still read newspapers)or your favorite news portal:

Public Wary of Deficit, Economic Intervention
Historic Overhaul of Finance Rules

The *public* is wary of the deficit and economic intervention? I'm part of the public, so I guess I had better be wary too. And a big change in the rules? Better keep up with that one too. I earn, save, borrow, spend, and invest money, so I'd better find out about any changes in the rules.

Truth is, headlines like this have become part of daily life. Sure, a few years ago, headlines about GDP growth or trade deficits or interest rates were mostly background noise, to be ignored unless you were an economist. Things were going pretty well. We had money to spend, everything was growing just a little each year, our retirement accounts were growing steadily, our jobs were reasonably safe . . .

And then it happened.

It is the Great Recession, the economic crisis—that big crisis of 2008–2009, the effects of which have lasted well into 2013, after years of good times. Good times? Not for everyone, but for a lot of us. During those times (remember when?) our homes earned more than we did. Those of us who earned any income at all—and most retirees—could borrow money cheaply and almost without any questions asked. We used our homes as ATMs. We could buy anything we wanted, and who cared about the debt, or deficits, or inflation? That was covered too, because home prices and other investment prices were going up. But it all went "poof" starting in 2007. The speeding locomotive of real estate prices, supported by lax lending practices, suddenly went into reverse.

Much to our surprise, everything turned out to be connected to everything else. The rest is history. And it's a history that continues to play out, and will play out for years to come.

Some of you may have taken that boring, senior-level "Econ" class in high school. You may have a rudimentary understanding of economics from that or some other class or from an uncle or grandparent who got a kick out of telling you about growing up as a kid during the Great Depression. You may have learned something along the way about supply and demand. You understood the difference between macroeconomics and microeconomics. You know that a good economy means a strong GDP and low unemployment. You have an idea that when those things are going well, you're more likely to have some spending money in your wallet and that your 401(k) and other retirement plans will grow at least a bit. You know enough to fear inflation and that someday—inevitably—there will be yet another recession, who knows when or why. But that's about it.

Now those relatively basic economic concepts have been set upon their ear. During the Great Recession, those news flashes were about "deleveraging," "deflation," "credit default swaps," "asset-backed securities," "hedge funds," and "globalization." I think we'd all agree—these were alarming words to hear even as we heard them day in and day out. As the economy jerked into reverse, we had the "impossible" collapse of big names like Bear Stearns and Lehman Brothers and the near-collapse of the banking system itself, with threats of twenty-dollar bills being no longer available in your local ATM machine. We got "medicine" in the form of unprecedented federal bailouts—the so-called "TARP" bailout of $700 *billion* given to all those "too big to fail" lending institutions (almost all of which has been paid back, by the way). Even as the economy mends, the Federal Reserve chairman Ben Bernanke and his equivalents at the European and Japanese central banks continue to do what's possible to stimulate their economies, although now the news is about "tapering"— that is, in plain English, reducing—these efforts. Our president and other world leaders talk about the economy constantly— good news or bad. No doubt, it's a complex, interconnected, and fast-paced world of change.

Before the Great Recession, the powers that be at the Federal Reserve, the SEC, and elsewhere for many years seemed to have control over things—if the economy went a little cool, they could stimulate it back to life; when it ran a little hot, they could cool it. They spoke of the "Goldilocks economy"—not too hot, not too cold. The medicine worked. Everyone *expected* it to work. However, in the past ten years, and especially during the crisis years of the Great Recession, the patient became less responsive to the usual medicine. So what's the good doctor to do? Increase the dosage, naturally. That meant lower interest rates and greater financial stimulus for longer periods of time. As of mid-2013, the Fed was still injecting $85 billion a month into the economy through bond purchases, keeping interest rates artificially low in an end-run effort to stimulate the economy and employment. Unfortunately, the "side effects"—the unintended consequences—could include a bond bubble or another real estate bubble, and many are worried today about catching a deadly inflationary virus as we move forward. Too, the stock market has advanced to new all-time highs anticipating the recovery, but how much of this recovery is "real" versus a response to artificial stimulus, that is, printing money? We may have solved some of the problems and dealt with some of the tough questions, but there is still a lot more to deal with.

Bottom line: It seems as if the more you know, the more you don't know, and since this stuff messes with your future, you'd better learn what's going on. So that's why the second edition of *101 Things Everyone Should Know about Economics* comes to the table once again at just the right time.

This book is not a crash course on economics, although some may decide to use it that way. Most definitely it isn't a textbook. Instead, it is intended to provide a handy reference to the very real concepts and terms in use in today's economy. It connects things you read about and hear about to things you need to know about and do. Or *not* do. It's more than a study guide for your economic life. It is intended to help you understand how economic concepts affect *you*. It is intended to help you make sense of what is good for you and bad for you, both now and in the future. It is intended to help you ask the right questions and ultimately take the right actions.

By no means is this book, like so many other books and articles you read, designed to help you get rich or earn more money or even save money. And, very importantly, this guide is not meant to help you understand just *today's* economy and its opportunities and pitfalls. This book is meant to help you be more knowledgeable, more aware, and more *prepared* going forward. Prepared to recognize the next crisis. Prepared to deal with it. Prepared to come out better than you did the last time. Prepared to come out better than you otherwise would have.

That preparation is important. Today's schools turn out graduates at all levels prepared to handle a career, perhaps multiple careers. But they still don't—much to our detriment—offer preparation for economic life. Even the "home economics" courses of the 1950s are gone; there is virtually nothing to help you live prudently or efficiently or economically, save for the vast assortment of books and magazines that tell you where to put your money *this* year. I believe a more basic understanding is necessary before you can trust yourself to make the right decisions. Today's education and media leave a huge gap in that area. *101 Things Everyone Should Know about Economics, 2nd Edition* is the fastest, friendliest, and most effective way to fill the gap.

THE ECONOMY IN SEVEN STEPS

Whether it's a book or a business presentation, I believe any complex topic can be broken down into between three and seven important pieces. That principle applies to this edition, as well as the first. The first chapter acts a refresher to common economic terms and then the remaining seven discuss the 101 economic concepts. I describe the concept, fast facts, what you should know, and why you should care about it. Common sense, start to finish. Beyond the first chapter, here is how the book is laid out:

- *Chapter 2: Economy and Economic Cycles.* A look at the economy as a whole as well as its current condition. This chapter offers a little bit of history, with special focus on the ups and downs, the booms and busts, why they happen, and how they affect you.

- *Chapter 3: Money, Prices, and Interest Rates.* What money is, what it does, and what happens to it, including inflation, deflation, and stagflation, and the cost of money—interest rates and the dynamics around them.
- *Chapter 4: Banks and Central Banking.* Once we understand money, it's time to learn about banks—the different kinds of banks and how the banking system works, with special emphasis on the Federal Reserve and its relationship to the banks and the economy at large.
- *Chapter 5: Government and Government Programs.* With the basic system outlined, who are the big government players in the economy, and what do they do? What are the most important laws and policies, why are they there, and how do they affect us?
- *Chapter 6: Economic Schools and Tools.* From government and government policy, we take another step toward the "big picture." What are the major schools of thought for managing or guiding the economy? How do they work? How do they explain what has happened, what should happen, or what's going to happen with our economy?
- *Chapter 7: Finance and Financial Markets.* The first six chapters covered the "macro" world. But what about all those things that happened on Wall Street that got us into trouble? Yes, there are hundreds of books about the stock market and Wall Street. But do they explain how Wall Street concepts connect to the larger economy? Do they explain "collateralized debt obligations" in plain English? And what you need to know about the financial markets and "retail" financial people like broker-dealers and financial advisers? And what about all those terms you see daily about real estate? Is a stock market short sale the same

as a real estate short sale? This chapter explains the most important financial markets and instruments of today.

- *Chapter 8: Trade and International Economics*. What is globalization, and how will it affect you? What makes the dollar gain against the euro, or vice versa? And what about those trade deficits? How does (and should) foreign trade work in a "new" economy? And how will that affect your job, the cost of living, and your life?

In the nineteenth century, the historian Thomas Carlyle was the first to refer to economics as "the dismal science." (To be fair, Carlyle wasn't exactly a bundle of laughs himself.) Since then, economics has labored under the burden of descriptions like "boring," "complicated," and "dry."

It doesn't have to be that way, and I hope this book will convince you otherwise. Economics is about the most basic human activities: what we produce, how we produce it, and how we consume it. It's concerned, in other words, with human behavior—in fact, in recent years the field of behavioral economics has risen to prominence because of best-selling books like *Freakonomics, The Black Swan,* and *Predictably Irrational.*

In this book, we're interested in what different economic terms and concepts mean, and how they affect us. So, to rather freely adapt a phrase made popular in the movies: read on and prosper.

CHAPTER 1

The Basics

If you have taken an introductory economics course in college or have read a basic economics textbook, you can probably skip this chapter and go right to the next one. But if you want to refresh your grasp of basic economic terms, read on. Feel free, as you go through this book, to flip back to this chapter if you get confused by some of the terminology.

A GLOSSARY OF BASIC ECONOMIC TERMS

Asset. Something that is owned. For businesses, it can take the form of things such as factories, products, and equipment. Assets can also be intangibles such as patents, trademarks, and copyrights. These kinds of things often fall into the category of *intellectual property*, a concept that's the subject of a growing body of law. In the age of the Internet, determining the value of an intangible asset has grown very complicated, and is probably going to become more so in the future.

Broker. Someone who sells or buys things on behalf of other people. For example, a mortgage broker buys and sells mortgages. An insurance broker arranges the sale of insurance policies to clients, and so on. The term *brokerage firm* usually refers to a company that deals in stocks. Brokers often make recommendations to their clients about what to buy and sell, but ultimately the buy-or-sell decision rests with the client.

Capital. Originally, this word described one of the factors used to produce goods (the others included things like land and labor). In today's economy, "capital" generally refers to cash as well as to material goods like manufacturing equipment, tools, and so on. The term *financial capital* is used when talking about the monetary resources entrepreneurs use to create their products or services.

Competitive Advantage. It's the nature of capitalism that businesses compete against one another. Each one tries to find some special way of beating its rivals, something that makes it stand out. That something is competitive advantage (also sometimes called the *competitive edge*). This is one of the most valuable tools a company has to ensure its growth, and companies try to protect their competitive advantages from all rivals.

Consumer. Anyone who uses goods and services that companies produce. Consumers have become a major driving force in the U.S. economy, and companies compete fiercely for their business. To this end, they spend a lot of time analyzing consumers, trying to figure out their buying patterns, their psychology, and so on.

Credit. Money that's loaned to someone or something. Credit can be in the form of a mortgage, a car loan, a line of credit through a credit card, or any one of numerous other forms. When you have credit, that's money that has been loaned to you by someone else. If you're a *creditor*, you've loaned money to someone, and they'll have to pay it back to you, usually with interest.

Debt. Something you owe to someone else. Personal debt has become a huge issue in the United States in recent years, and many people, as a result of their exploding debt, have suffered *bankruptcies* and *foreclosures*. However, some debt can be good— for example, if it's used to buy something that will *produce* value (like a business asset) or increase in value over time (like certain real estate investments), or something that you need but will cost more in the future. Bad debt is when you purchase something you don't need and can't afford.

Elasticity. In the context of economics, the measure of the ability of an economy to change rapidly in response to circumstances. In a more technical sense, it's the ratio between the percentage change in two variables (for example, supply and price). For instance, if the price of a product rises slightly and immediately the demand for it falls dramatically, the product is said to have high elasticity. The price of a product such as gasoline, on the other hand, can rise quite a lot before demand drops substantially, so it's said to have low elasticity.

Entrepreneur. Someone who starts a business and takes responsibility for its success or failure. The term has also come to mean someone who shows enterprise, initiative, and daring in the business community. Even though many new businesses fail, we still respect those who are brave enough to follow their dreams. Small businesses, started and operated by entrepreneurs, represent

99 percent of all U.S. businesses, and for many they represent American capitalism in its purest form.

Forecast. An estimate of where the economy, a business, or some feature of either is going. Different government agencies, as well as nongovernmental organizations, make economic forecasts, some of which can affect the performance of the markets. Businesses use forecasts to plan their goals and budgets. Keep in mind, though, that a forecast is a guess. It's usually an educated guess, but still a guess.

Free Enterprise. An economic system in which markets and companies are privately owned and are free to compete against one another with minimal government restrictions. This is the system that exists in the United States. It's sometimes referred to as *laissez-faire capitalism* or *free-market capitalism*.

** hedge fund see page 184 - #72
* holding Company

Innovation. The process by which companies come up with new products and services. Often, companies' research and development (R&D) divisions take the lead in driving innovation. An innovation goes beyond an "invention" in that it becomes a product or service that people will buy—that is, there's a market for it. Some companies (for example, Apple and Google) have built their *competitive advantage* on innovation—often with "disruptive" innovations that really change markets, in contrast to just adding refinements to existing products or services.

Interest. The fee paid in order to use borrowed money. Essentially, this is the cost of obtaining credit. Interest is calculated as a percentage of the amount borrowed. This percentage is called the *interest rate*. There are many different kinds of interest, including *simple interest* and *compound interest*. Interest rates are closely tied to *credit risk*, which is the risk that an extended credit—that is, a

* company that controls other companies - usu. thru stock ownership - but usually does not engage directly in their productive operations

loan—will not be paid. In general, at a time of high credit risk, interest rates tend to go up, since creditors want to make sure they recoup their money. However, this isn't always the case.

Investor. Someone who puts money into a business in order to earn a return—that is, to make more money. Sometimes investors do this by loaning money to the entrepreneurs who are starting or running the business. More often, they do it by purchasing stock—an ownership stake—in the business. The basic point to keep in mind is that investors want to earn a return. The percentage of money they make in relation to their investment is called their *return on investment*, or *"ROI."*—see "Return on Investment."

Macroeconomics. As implied by the term "macro," the study of economics on a large scale: regional, national, or international economic trends and issues. Macroeconomists try to figure out what drives entire economic systems, and what impact these systems have on each other.

Microeconomics. Basically the opposite of macroeconomics. Microeconomics studies economic movement on a smaller scale—for individual businesses or even on the level of individual households. Microeconomists also study the behavior of companies and regions to understand how these units are allocating their resources and responding to pressures from above and below. A microeconomist might also study the behavior of a single product or product type.

Monopoly. A single company or individual controlling an entire product or service. In the nineteenth century, monopolies were fairly common in America (Standard Oil, for example). Throughout the late nineteenth and twentieth centuries, many of them were broken up by legislation, starting with the Sherman Antitrust Act of 1890. Today, government agencies review mergers in an attempt to prevent the formation of monopolies. In recent years, several monopoly-related cases have received a great deal of attention, most famously involving Microsoft, and have also entered the conversation with major wireless carriers, the oil industry, and other mergers.

Mortgage. The security for the money you owe to a lender. When you take out a mortgage, you borrow money and give the lender an interest in a property to secure the repayment of the debt. When you've satisfied the terms of the mortgage (that is, when you've paid the debt), the interest of the lender in your property will be returned to you. If you don't repay the debt, the lender can *foreclose* on the property.

Outsourcing. The increasingly common practice of contracting people outside an organization to perform work that used to be done by people within a company. Outsourcing has grown massively to include everything from call centers and customer service to information technology services. Many American companies are outsourcing overseas to countries such as India, China, and Mexico, where labor costs and other costs of doing business are lower.

* Portfolio

Publicly Held Company. A company that's registered with the Securities and Exchange Commission and whose stock is traded on the open market, where it can be bought and sold by the public. In a *privately held company*, on the other hand, stock is held by a relatively small number of shareholders, who don't trade it openly. Often these are family or friends of the owner. Eventually, the company may hold an *initial public offering (IPO)* and issue stock shares on the open market. After the company registers with the SEC, it becomes a public company.

* Securities, commercial paper held by a financial institution

Productivity. A measure of efficiency. It's often expressed as the ratio of units to labor hours (a company produces two thousand pairs of shoes per hour, for example). Productivity is one element that's factored into studies of *economic growth*. In general, industries try to increase productivity through technological innovation and other methods.

Profit Margin. A company's net income divided by sales. It's a basic measure of profitability, one that companies look at closely each year. Companies also look at metrics like revenue, but they aren't considered as significant as profit margin. After all, a company can increase its revenue by selling more products, but if the production costs increase (for example, because of a rise in the price of raw materials or labor), the company isn't really making any more money.

* Proprietary trading - see p. 82

Return on Investment. A measure of how much money an investor gets back relative to the amount invested. It's sometimes called the *rate of return* or the *rate of profit*. Many people make decisions about investment or other financial activities based on their calculation of ROI.

* securities

Venture Capital. Money that's put into new businesses by outside investors. Venture capitalists tend to look for high-potential startup companies that can grow quickly and provide a strong return on investment. Family and friends who lend money for startups are sometimes referred to as *angel capital*. In some cases, venture capitalists anticipate that the company will grow to a certain stage and then be sold for a profit, and they'll reap a rich reward. Alternately, the company may be successful in its initial public offering and see its stock rise dramatically in value. Many large companies such as Google and more recently Facebook started out this way.

Volcker Rule - see p. 82

** securities - stocks, bonds - s'thing given in fulfillment of a debt

CHAPTER 2

Economy and Economic Cycles

We start with the economy. Not a big surprise in a book titled *101 Things Everyone Should Know about Economics.* By way of definition, the economy is a *system* to allocate scarce resources to provide the things we need. That system includes the production, distribution, consumption, and exchange of goods and services. It is about what we do as a society to support ourselves, and about how we exchange what we do to take advantage of our skills, land, labor, and capital.

Of course, that definition is a bit oversimplified. The economy is really a fabulously complicated mechanism that hums along at high speed—the speed of light with today's technology—to facilitate production and consumption. The economy itself is fairly abstract, but touches us as individuals with things like income, consumption, savings, and investments, or more concretely, with money, food, cars, fuel, and savings for college.

One could only wish ours was a "steady state" economy—that it would always provide exactly what we need when we needed it. Unfortunately, it isn't so simple. The economy is directly influenced by a huge, disconnected aggregation of individual decisions. There is no "central" planning for the economy (yes, it's been tried, but doesn't work for a variety of reasons), although governments, central banks, and other economic authorities can influence its direction. Because the economy functions on millions of small decisions, the economy is subject to error—overproduction and overconsumption, for example. Take these errors, add in a few unforeseen events, and the result is that economies go through cycles of strength and weakness.

The first fifteen entries describe the economy, economic cycles, economic results, and some of the measures economists use to measure economic activity.

1. INCOME

Income is the money we receive in order to buy what we need when we need it. Economists look at income in several different ways—including where it comes from, how much is earned, and how much of what is earned can really be spent. Income includes the following money flows: wages to labor, profit to businesses and enterprise, interest to capital, and rent to land.

What You Should Know

Income is what people earn through either direct labor or as owners of investments. The amount of income we earn as individuals and families connects to the economy's prosperity and strength. It dictates how much we can ultimately spend and the value we bring to the economy as a whole. The amount of income earned collectively as a country determines the economic health of a nation and of groups within it.

Economists look at *national income* (covered further under #4 GDP), *per capita income* (income generated per person), and *household income* (how much income is generated by the average household). In all but the worst times, incomes should rise as people accomplish more by becoming more skilled and productive at their jobs and in their businesses. Economists also speak of *real* income increases—that is, increases adjusted for inflation, as opposed to *nominal* increases, which represent the raw numbers but not necessarily true income growth.

Economists also consider *disposable income*, or the amount of income actually available for individuals and families to spend after taxes. Disposable income is a truer indicator of how much purchasing power we really have, and how much of that purchasing power will ultimately be available to drive the economy and create more income.

The Census Bureau measures income annually through the American Community Survey. Income figures are published in the financial press and can be seen in greater detail on the U.S. Census Bureau's website: *www.census.gov/hhes/www/income/income.html*.

You can see how income is distributed among different population groups or states, as well as overall income growth. The annual press release will contain statements like: "Real median household income in the United States declined by 1.5 percent between 2010 and 2011, reaching $50,054." The decline in median household incomes—some 8.1 percent since 2007—has been persistent, and is one of the reasons that our leaders are so concerned about the economy these days.

Why You Should Care

Most of you probably care more about your personal income than that of the nation or others around you! Your own income ultimately determines your purchasing power and is a key factor in your overall quality of life. If your income isn't increasing—or worse, if it is decreasing—you know that's not a good thing, and you might have to adjust your way of life.

Watching published income figures helps you keep tabs on the ups and downs of the economy. By itself that may or may not interest you, depending on your profession or general level of interest in national success. However, if you track national, household, and per capita income *changes* and compare them with your own, you can see whether you're gaining or losing ground.

Income changes can also be useful as a measuring stick for other economic factors, like growth in asset prices. During the real estate boom, for example, home prices far outpaced gains in income. Smart economists knew this couldn't last forever. Either incomes had to rise (to keep pace) or home prices had to stabilize or fall (to allow incomes to catch up). So watching gains in income can be a good test to make sure other economic changes make sense.

See also: #2 Consumption, #4 Gross Domestic Product (GDP), and #14 Distribution of Income and Wealth.

2. CONSUMPTION

Quite simply, consumption is what we, in aggregate, consume. And like income, the measurement of consumption at a national level helps us understand whether the economy is getting weaker or stronger. As an individual, you have more control over consumption than income, so it's important to monitor your consumption to be certain you can make ends meet.

What You Should Know

Economists track *personal consumption expenditures (PCE)*. As the term implies, PCE represents funds spent on goods and services for individual consumption. "Goods" breaks down into *durable* goods—goods expected to have a useful life greater than three years, like cars and lawnmowers—and *nondurable* goods like food, paper products, cleaning supplies, and so forth. Personal consumption expenditures exist in addition to private business investment, providing goods and services for export, and government consumption of goods and services.

The Bureau of Economic Analysis (*www.bea.gov*) monitors and publishes PCE reports; the Bureau of Labor Statistics (*www.bls.gov*) gives longer histories and projections for PCE. Since consumption accounts for some 71 percent of the total U.S. economy, a small change in PCE can signal a big change in prosperity ahead.

Why You Should Care

At a national level, during the boom years prior to the Great Recession, low interest rates, easy credit, and low-cost imported goods combined to cause a consumption bubble of massive proportions; the Great Recession was in part an unwinding of that bubble. Savings rates (covered in the next entry) went from negative to moderately positive as consumers became more conservative. This caution has brought consumption back to more sustainable levels—that is, somewhat less than income and more in line with income growth.

That's a good thing on a national basis. The key for you as an individual is to make sure your own PCE is in line with your income and income growth. And if you're an investor, monthly PCE reports can give you an insight to where the economy is headed.

3. SAVING AND INVESTMENT

The personal saving rate is defined, very simply, as the percent of personal income that is not consumed. In specific economic terms, it is personal disposable income minus personal consumption expenditures. In real-world terms, it's money you don't spend today but instead put aside to spend tomorrow.

Investment, on the other hand, is an allocation of goods or capital not to be used just for current but also future production. Over time, when an economy is in balance, saving should equal investment; that is, the money, or wealth, put aside should be invested, or used, for future consumption.

Granted, that sounds a bit complicated and theoretical. As a practical matter, it's more interesting to look at saving as it has really occurred over time. It's also more interesting to think about how saving and investment should occur in your own household.

What You Should Know

First, it's important to distinguish "saving" from "savings." Saving is the setting aside of surplus funds—that is, what you don't spend. Savings refers to the actual accounts, like your savings accounts, in which you do it. The level of "saving," not "savings," is what's really important for you and for the economy as a whole.

Consumer saving, until recently, had been on the skids for quite some time. For many years we were a nation of savers: in the 1960s saving was 6 to 10 percent of income, and rose to a level as high as 14 percent briefly in the recessionary period of 1975 (yes, saving rises during economic hardship; see #35 Paradox of Thrift).

In the late 1970s, saving rates started to decline because of high inflation rates—people needed more of their income to meet expenses and came to expect the purchasing power of their savings to diminish. Saving rates fell back to the 8 to 10 percent range, still healthy by today's standards. The 1982 recession increased it to 12 percent; that peak foreshadowed a long, slow decline into the 6 to 8 percent range by the late 1980s, down to 2 percent in the late 1990s, and hitting negative territory by 2005. It has hovered near zero since then; however, in the aftermath of the Great Recession, the savings rate rose to about 5 percent, as people feared for their jobs and incomes, and has settled a bit to the 3 percent range. That sudden return to saving, ironically, hampered the recovery (see #35 Paradox of Thrift).

Why You Should Care

Until the Great Recession hit, most Americans fell into a trap of increased consumption, the prioritization of "now" over the future. We felt the "wealth effect" (see #15) of higher house prices, cheaper goods mainly from China, stable incomes, and strong marketing messages. Saving took a back seat, despite dire warnings about the future of Social Security and retirement. The combination of weak income growth, unemployment, and asset price declines brought a sudden end to the party. The message, of course: prudent Americans should choose the path of sustained wealth, placing savings as first priority and buying only what we can afford. You should invest those savings for returns in the future, as should society as a whole.

4. GROSS DOMESTIC PRODUCT (GDP)

Gross domestic product is the sum total of all goods and services produced in an economy. As it measures the market value of all final goods and services produced by a nation, it is a fundamental indicator of an economy's performance. It is highly correlated with personal incomes and standard of living. It can be looked at as a true measure of the *value added* by an economy.

What You Should Know

The calculation of GDP boils down to a sum of four items: *Personal consumption* plus *total personal and business investment* plus *public or government consumption* plus *net exports* (exports minus imports). It is thus a measure of what is consumed today (consumption) plus what is put aside for tomorrow (investment) plus our net sales to others around the world. That combined figure in turn roughly represents the income we as a nation produce from all of those activities.

Economists track both the size and the change in GDP. The U.S. GDP in 2012 was just over $14.5 trillion, but with the effects of the Great Recession, the average annual growth rate dropped from 3.2 percent (1997–2007) to an average of 0.7 percent from 2005 to 2010. More recently, it has returned to a still rather anemic 1.5 to 2 percent. GDP dropped 6.3 percent in the fourth quarter of 2008, one of the sharpest declines on record, and a true measure of the severity of the Great Recession. At that time it should be noted that other economies fared worse—Germany's GDP went down 14.4 percent, Japan's 15.2 percent, and Mexico's declined by 21.5 percent in the same period. However, their base GDPs are much smaller, so the value lost in the decline was less.

The breakdown of U.S. GDP components (from 2012) is also interesting:

Personal consumption	71%
Personal and business investment	15%

Public, or government, consumption	17%
Exports	13%
Imports	-16%

The good news is that exports have increased about 2 percent since 2008, while imports dropped about 1 percent (influenced in a large measure by reduced dependence on foreign oil). Also, the public/government consumption share has declined about 2 percent, signaling less reliance on that sector. But dependence on consumption still remains high, as the following figures for China will show:

Personal consumption	35%
Personal and business investment	48%
Public, or government consumption	13%
Exports	30%
Imports	-26%

China, in contrast to the United States, is foregoing current consumption to build for the future, although the trade balance has shifted about 5 percent away from exports and toward imports—perhaps bad for China, but good for the rest of the world.

The GDP is also an important measure of *standard of living*. Economists measure GDP per capita—that is, per person in a nation. Here, the U.S. at $47,150 (World Bank figure from 2012) is on solid footing, although not at the top of the pack (twelve nations, including Norway, Denmark, Australia, and Qatar, are ahead on this measure). As well, economic wealth isn't the only component of standard of living; the less measurable safety, health, leisure time, and climate go beyond GDP per capita as components of true living standards (though these are sometimes separated out as components of *quality of living*).

Why You Should Care

The GDP is the broadest measure of the country's overall economic health, and it defines the economic "pie" you ultimately enjoy a slice of. If it is healthy and growing, times are good; if it is stagnant or declining, it will most likely affect your standard of living, sooner or later.

5. UNEMPLOYMENT AND UNEMPLOYMENT RATES

Most of you have a good idea of what unemployment is—especially when you don't have a job! Economists take the same view, but add the conditions that unemployed people are not only without a job but are also available to work and are actively seeking employment. The unemployment rate is the percentage of the work force that is currently out of a job and is unable to find one, but is actively looking.

What You Should Know

Economists closely watch the unemployment rate as a signal of overall economic health. High unemployment is a sign that an economy is weak currently and will remain so. Why? Obviously, if people are losing jobs, demand is most likely falling, as are incomes and purchasing power. When people lose jobs, they can afford less, home foreclosures rise, they can save less for retirement, and their future becomes more grim in general.

Economists also recognize that there is no such thing as a true, 100 percent, full-employment economy. Some unemployment is *structural*; that is, created by changing job requirements—there simply aren't as many jobs for autoworkers or office clerks these days. Some is _frictional_, caused by the natural changes businesses make and that people make to their lives, moving from one place to another. Some is _seasonal_, the result of a decline in certain jobs that are tied to particular times of the year (for example, sales clerks in retail stores during the Christmas holidays). As a result, economists suggest that an unemployment rate of about 4 percent represents "full employment."

As you can see from Figure 2.1, unemployment rates reached an all-time low during World War II and a substantial all-time high in 1933. The numbers for that year were astounding: 25 percent overall for the work force; 37 percent for nonfarm workers (see #6 Recessions and #7 Depressions). Aside from those periods, the unemployment rate in good times decreases to about 4 percent and surges toward 10 percent in recessions, including 1982 and the most recent in 2009. More recently, unemployment rates have ticked back downward to the mid-7 percent range. Typically, when unemployment rates exceed 7 percent or so, governments go into action to stimulate the economy (see #58 Chicago or Monetarist School, and #57 Keynesian School).

Figure 2.1 U.S. Unemployment Rates, 1890–2011

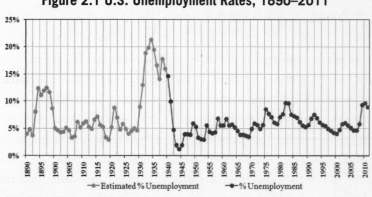

Source: Bureau of Labor Statistics

Why You Should Care

Obviously, when unemployment is on the rise, it suggests a reduction in business activity, which means you should be more fearful for your job as well. You should do whatever you can to make yourself more employable, including building new skills or becoming more indispensable on your job, by building expertise and credibility within your own organization. You should also develop contingency plans, including savings cushions and prospects for perhaps doing your job as an independent contractor. Long-term employment with big companies still happens, but is less the norm than ten or twenty years ago; it has become more of a "free agent" economy, and you should hold nothing back in becoming part of it. Aside from keeping an eye on the unemployment rate in order to protect your job, it's a smart way to monitor the pulse of the economy, which will affect your investments, your company if you're a small-business owner, and your tax revenues if you're in the public sector.

6. RECESSIONS

The U.S. National Bureau of Economic Research defines a recession as a period with "a significant decline in economic activity spread across the country, lasting more than a few months, normally visible in real GDP growth, real personal income, employment (nonfarm payrolls), industrial production, and wholesale-retail sales." During that time business profits typically decline as well. As a result, public-sector tax revenue also falls.

What You Should Know

Many call it a recession simply when a country's GDP declines two calendar quarters in a row, or when the unemployment rate rises 1.5 percent in less than twelve months.

Technical definitions aside, perhaps Harry Truman had the best definition of a recession, and how it differs from a depression: "It's a recession when your neighbor loses his job; it's a depression when you lose yours."

Recessions can be notoriously hard to forecast. For instance, how many really predicted the Great Recession, and especially its severity? When things are going well, we tend to become complacent, even optimistic, about the idea that anything can go wrong. We've grown accustomed to federal government intervention to prevent recessions by lowering interest rates and taking other measures to stimulate the economy (see #8 Business Cycle). Even the markets can't tell us much; as economist Paul Samuelson famously stated: "The stock market has forecasted nine of the last five recessions."

The National Bureau of Economic Research, the U.S. government organization generally responsible for identifying recessions, has noted ten recessions since World War II. As you can see from the table, recessions are generally short in duration—lasting less than a year—and typically happen about twice a decade.

The most recent of these, the so-called Great Recession, was also the largest since World War II, with a drop in GDP from peak to trough of 5.1 percent. By contrast, from August 1929 through March 1933, during the Great Depression, the GDP dropped 26.7 percent—hence "Depression" instead of "Recession."

Table 2.1 U.S. Recessions 1945–2012

Occurrence	Duration
November 1948–October 1949	11 months
July 1953–May 1954	10 months
August 1957–April 1958	8 months
April 1960–February 1961	10 months
December 1969–November 1970	11 months
November 1973–March 1975	16 months
January 1980–July 1980	6 months
July 1981–November 1982	16 months
July 1990–March 1991	8 months
March 2001–November 2001	8 months
December 2007–June 2009	18 months

Source: U.S. Bureau of Economic Research

Why You Should Care

Recessions mean less for everybody, and unless you have a pile of money or are in a business largely immune to downturns, you should prepare to make adjustments when recession clouds start to gather. Warning signs include changes in the employment rate, an excess of debt, or "irrational exuberance" in some or all markets (like dot-com stocks in 2000 and real estate in 2006). You should learn to recognize when times are good, and use those times to save some money.

You should also watch to make sure your standard of living is matched to the worst, not to the best, of times. In good times, avoid allowing your lifestyle to consume all of your income, and worse, to put you into debt. If you do, you'll have the flexibility to get through the bad times.

7. DEPRESSIONS

In economics, a depression is a sharp, protracted, and sustained downturn in economic activity, usually crossing borders as a worldwide event. It is more severe, and usually longer, than a recession, which is seen as a more-or-less normal feature of the business cycle (see #8 Business Cycle).

Depressions are usually associated with large collapses in business, bankruptcies, sharply reduced trade, very large increases in unemployment, failures in the banking and credit system, and a general crisis mentality and panic among the population, big corporations, and policymakers. Depressions can cause severe economic dislocations, including deflation (see #19 Deflation) and the wholesale demise of certain industries.

Of course, the Great Depression is the granddaddy of all depressions, lasting, by most accounts, from the 1929 stock market crash, which triggered subsequent banking failures and spread to the larger economy, all the way to World War II.

What You Should Know

To give an idea of the severity of depressions, the unemployment rate during the Great Depression went from 3 percent in 1929 to 25 percent in 1933 (37 percent for nonfarm workers). In some cities with a large factory base, it rose as high as 80 percent.

The good news is that depressions don't happen often. As of 2012, there have only been three "depression" events in U.S. history: the Great Depression in the 1930s and two less severe panics in 1837 and 1873.

A long and large economic expansion that turned into a speculative bubble fueled by borrowing and debt preceded all three depressions. Those who borrow too much fail first, as they cannot service their debt, and that causes a rise in bankruptcies and asset prices to fall, leading to a vicious circle of debt-unwinding known as *deleveraging* (see #9 Deleveraging).

The challenge of the government is to intervene effectively to help out the economy. The Great Depression led to a significant banking panic. As banks failed, the government adopted a "laissez-faire" mentality, letting weaker elements be flushed from the system. This approach is good in theory, but it accelerated the panic. A misguided attempt to protect American business through trade tariffs failed miserably and made the problem worse.

Government may intervene, but history shows it has yet to do so effectively. By the time the U.S. government stepped in, it was too late; markets and businesses starved first for credit and then for customers had shut down. The government started stimulus programs to put people to work, moved away from the gold standard, devalued the dollar to make U.S. goods more competitive internationally, and passed legislation to protect the public from such calamities in the future. It was a very long and rocky ten years.

Why You Should Care

The Great Recession had some of the earmarks of a depression in the making, with severe stress on the banking and credit system and sharp rises in unemployment. But the many safeguards, like deposit insurance, Social Security, unemployment insurance (see these entries in Chapter 5), and various other forms of government intervention made a downturn of 1930s proportions seem unlikely. That said, you, as a person in charge of your finances, must always recognize the possibility—not probability but *possibility*—that such an event could occur, and keep your finances protected against such a downturn.

8. BUSINESS CYCLE

The term "business cycle" describes a more-or-less normal flow of American and world business activity over time from strength to weakness and back to strength. "Boom" conditions describe strong business growth throughout the economy, while a "bust" occurs when the economy gets tired, or some intervening event occurs that sends the tide the other way. Booms and busts have occurred throughout economic history, and naturally, one follows the other, but their pattern isn't identical or predictable.

What You Should Know

Business cycles are natural and unavoidable, and arise out of the normal course of business. Government policy can smooth them or help them along, but it can't create or prevent them. Cycles arise from two primary factors: the imperfection of information and the evolution of technology and tastes.

Imperfection of information refers to the fact that business leaders don't have perfect information when they make decisions; they make too much, sell too little, and spend too much because they don't have perfect crystal balls. The evolution of tastes and technology, a constant through history but occurring ever faster, creates new markets and eliminates old ones.

These two elements cause businesses to overshoot, overcorrect, and otherwise make flawed decisions. In a boom, that can lead to overproduction and the assumption of excess debt and risk—which then leads to a bust. The business contraction that follows eventually reduces supply, cleans up excess debt, and starts business over with a clean slate toward another boom. Through increased spending and lowered interest rates, government policy helps the process along. Business cycles bring new things and clean old, obsolete businesses off the economic floor.

As William Poole, former Federal Reserve Bank of St. Louis chairman, eloquently put it: "The world we live in is uncertain and cyclical because the U.S. economy is dynamic, inventive, experimental, and entrepreneurial. Some ideas are carried to excess, we discover after the fact. Look at the littered landscape of dead railroads, dead auto companies, and dead airlines to illustrate the point."

Why You Should Care

Booms and busts are a natural part of your financial life. If you have a steady job, you might not have to worry too much, but it's always good to be aware of what's going on and how it might affect your behavior and your finances. People tend to become "giddy" during booms, taking on more risk without realizing they're doing so (as in buying overpriced homes, no money down, during the real estate boom). To keep from getting in over your head financially, you should always tune your finances to the bust; then the boom will feel that much better.

9. DELEVERAGING

Deleveraging refers to the tendency for individuals and corporations to get rid of debt in a forced, untimely manner during a bust cycle, or recession. It is the opposite of adding leverage—that is, borrowing more and using those funds to buy assets, where perhaps one dollar of your own is matched to nine borrowed dollars to buy something worth ten dollars. The 9:1 leverage ratio is nice, so long as the asset continues to be worth ten dollars or more, but the first dollar lost is your dollar if asset prices go down. To deleverage, you would pay off your nine-dollar debt as quickly as possible to reduce your risk of loss.

What You Should Know

Desperate to repair the damage inflicted on their balance sheets by debt, financial institutions will sell assets during a deleveraging cycle. When they sell assets, guess what? Prices go down. That actually makes it worse, starting a vicious circle as forced sales push asset prices down further. This then spreads to more companies, more individuals, more balance sheets. Soon the government is left with the only balance sheet strong enough to keep buying.

The deleveraging that hit in late 2008 was severe and was a major contributor to the Great Recession. Banks laden with mortgage-backed securities were forced to sell them to make good on deposits by their customers; that selling process further cut the value of those securities, which were nearly impossible to value in the first place. As stock prices fell, hedge funds (see #72 Hedge Fund) were caught flatfooted by investors requiring redemptions, since the funds were borrowing money to juice their returns. Therefore, the hedge funds were forced to sell assets to meet those redemptions and pay down debt. That made stock prices fall faster than they otherwise would have.

Why You Should Care

The point is to never get into a situation where you have to pay back debt in a panic. The assets you borrowed to buy will be worth less, and it will be that much harder to raise the money you need to pay off the debt. Best place to be: no debt at all. If you have debt, it should be only in assets you would be unlikely to sell in most situations (for example, your house), and with interest and principal payments well within your budget even in tougher times

10. MISERY INDEX

Sometimes it helps to put the economic data you see, hear, and read about together and in context with a single indicator or two. It's like taking all the weather data—temperature, humidity, precipitation probability, wind speed—and coming up with "it's going to be a nice day." Or, in this case, a bad day.

Some years ago, the economist Arthur Okun did this for us by creating a "misery index." By adding together the inflation rate (see #18 Inflation) and the unemployment rate (see #5 Unemployment and Unemployment Rates), you arrive at the misery index.

What You Should Know

Taking the index apart for a moment, you can see that high inflation with low unemployment, or high unemployment with low inflation, is bad, but not as bad as things could be. The combination of high inflation *and* high unemployment occur in the unusual and painful combination of *stagflation* (see #20 Stagflation). This is the signal the misery index sends when it is at its highest.

It's interesting to track the misery index through history, specifically through the times and policies of the various presidents. As you can see in Table 2.2, the misery index varies to a great degree during presidential terms, hitting an all-time high of 21.98 percent at one point during the Carter years as inflation hit double-digit levels at the end of his administration. This "misery" helps explain his loss to Ronald Reagan in 1980.

Table 2.2 Misery Index by President

President	Period	Average Misery Index	Overall Rank
Harry Truman	1948–52	7.78	5
Dwight Eisenhower	1953–60	6.26	1 (best)
John F. Kennedy	1961–62	7.14	3
Lyndon Johnson	1963–68	6.77	2
Richard Nixon	1969–73	10.57	7
Gerald Ford	1974–76	16.0	11
Jimmy Carter	1977–80	16.26	12 (worst)
Ronald Reagan	1981–88	12.19	10
George H. W. Bush	1989–92	10.68	9
Bill Clinton	1993–2000	7.80	4
George W. Bush	2001–08	8.11	6
Barack Obama	2009–present	10.48	8

Source: miseryindex.us

The misery index has been relatively stable since the mid-1980s, owing largely to government focus on moderating inflation rates and an absence of large oil price shocks. The sharp rise in the unemployment rate during the Great Recession drove the index over 10 during the Obama administration, but a low inflation rate has kept it from tracking higher—at least so far. The Federal Reserve has generally leaned toward controlling inflation at the expense of short-term rises in unemployment, as inflation—once imbedded in the economy—is more difficult to eliminate (see #18 Inflation). But more recently, the Fed has become more aggressive on unemployment, and has made it the target for most of its operations. The inflation rate is vulnerable but has stayed in check—in part due to moderated energy and commodity prices, and in part due to continued slack demand resulting from unemployment. The next administration may well see a misery index around 10, but with higher inflation and lower unemployment as components.

Why You Should Care

In most situations, economic policy is a tradeoff between inflation (a result of economic strength) and unemployment (a result of economic weakness). Policymakers make course corrections between the two in trying to smooth out the business cycle (see #8 Business Cycle). A high misery index indicates a loss of control—that is, some part of the policy arsenal isn't working for one reason or another. That's a sign of trouble ahead.

11. CONSUMER CONFIDENCE

Economists can look at actual numbers all they want, but most of those numbers simply reflect what's already happened. Since such a large part of the economy is driven by consumer spending (see #4 Gross Domestic Product), and since economists like to see where things are going, many pay close attention to so-called consumer confidence measures. These findings follow and record how optimistic consumers are about the overall economy as well as their personal finances.

What You Should Know

Consumer confidence is a measure of perception, not actual economic activity. As a result, it can only be measured by survey—that is, by asking a carefully collected sample of people how they are feeling about their financial health and the economy overall.

There are two dominant measures of consumer confidence today: the Consumer Confidence Index (CCI) published by the nonprofit Conference Board and the University of Michigan's Index of Consumer Sentiment (ICS). Both are revised and published monthly.

The CCI is based on a monthly survey of five thousand U.S. households. The survey, tabulated for each of the nine census regions and for the country as a whole, consists of just five questions designed to tease out consumer insights about the following:

1. Current business conditions
2. Business conditions for the next six months
3. Current employment conditions
4. Employment conditions for the next six months
5. Expectations of total family income for the next six months

The results are compared to similar results from 1985, considered a standard to measure against because the economy at that time was in the exact middle of a business cycle. The base is set at 100 and all other results are presented as an index versus the 1985 base. So a reading of less than 100 indicates consumer pessimism and a reading above 100 shows consumer optimism.

To put everything into perspective, at the depth of the recent recession in February 2009, CCI reported consumer confidence at 25.8; economists and the media rejoiced when it jumped to 40.8 by April of that year, still a very pessimistic figure compared to the 100 base and a reading of 144.7 in January 2000. More recently, in 2012, the index has ranged between 61.3 and 73.1; in 2013, between 58.4 and 76.2.

The ICS is similar to the CCI and asks five similar but not identical questions. The time horizon is different; respondents are asked to project economic conditions and their own finances for the next twelve months rather than six. As perhaps a truer proxy of expected behavior, they are asked about their attitude toward buying specific major household items, like automobiles.

Why You Should Care

A high CCI and ICS suggest good things ahead for the economy; a low reading reflects consumer pessimism and suggests a downturn. They are leading indicators of your own economic success. You may also want to measure your own "consumer confidence" against the readings—if you're feeling worse about things while others are feeling better, that's a sign that you need to consider some changes.

12. PRODUCTIVITY

Productivity is the amount of economic output, or value, derived from a unit of labor, land, or capital (the three generic forms of economic input).

What You Should Know

Productivity is a measure of economic efficiency, and especially the effectiveness of new technologies as applied to the economy. New technologies have allowed people to produce more and more, faster and faster, as anyone in today's data- and communication-intensive world knows. But productivity increases based on technology aren't new; the advent of railroads, electricity, and communications technologies have been revolutionizing commerce for years.

What's most interesting is the increasing pace of technological innovation. It is still sobering to think that widespread personal computer availability and use has only occurred over the past twenty-five years; universal, browser-driven Internet use, and mobile phone use, for that matter, is less than twenty years old. It's hard to imagine a business world without these things.

Economists study productivity in part because it's an important factor in keeping a lid on inflation. As an economy grows, it typically adds inflationary pressure because the heightened demand for economic inputs drives prices higher. But when productivity increases—meaning more output can be generated with relatively less input—inflationary pressure is reduced. That fundamental was closely watched during the Federal Reserve's Greenspan years, as the Fed could stimulate the economy with low interest rates without necessarily triggering inflation. Increased productivity, due mainly to advancements in technology, was one of the reasons.

Incidentally, that gain in productivity didn't happen right away. For many years, economists recognized a *productivity paradox*, where the advent of technology tools did not necessarily spur productivity. This was the case in the late 1980s and early 1990s. In fact, some thought this new technology, especially computers, *hurt* productivity, since more resources were expended implementing the technology than producing output. Computer technology also increased the size of firms and bureaucracy, making both less manageable. The reality was that business hadn't learned to *use* the machines effectively at that point. However that's no longer the case, as U.S. productivity has been improving for years (though the rate of improvement has slowed in recent years). That, in fact, is one reason employment hasn't responded as well to economic stimulus as policymakers might have hoped—companies have figured out how to produce more stuff without hiring more people.

Why You Should Care

Everyone should strive for greater productivity. As the economy becomes more productive, the onus is on you to become more productive personally too—otherwise you're losing ground! When new technologies become available, it doesn't mean you *have to* use them, but you should at least familiarize yourself with them. Imagine where you would be if you refused to use PCs, e-mail, and mobile phones!

At the same time, if U.S. economic productivity went into a decline, that would be a bad sign for both economic growth and inflation. More resources would be consumed to produce the same amount of output, which would likely result in higher inflation, shortages, poor profit performance on the part of firms, and, ultimately, higher unemployment. With productivity, "turning back the clock" is a bad idea.

13. ECONOMIC INDICATORS

Economists love to measure things and are always looking for ways to gauge future economic trends. They have developed a set of *leading economic indicators*, measures of the economy designed to help us figure out "where the puck is going," as hockey great Wayne Gretzky would have put it. Economists also track a set of *lagging economic indicators* to measure where the economy has been, diagnose change, learn from it, and make better predictions for the future.

What You Should Know

Like the CCI, the Conference Board has put together a monthly index that combines ten different leading indicators, not surprisingly referred to as the Conference Board Leading Economic Index (LEI). Without going into details (although some are covered in this book), here are the ten leading indicators:

- Stock prices
- Index of consumer expectations
- Manufacturers' new orders for consumer goods
- Manufacturers' new orders for nondefense capital goods
- Average weekly manufacturing hours
- Interest rate spreads
- Index of supplier deliveries
- Initial claims for unemployment insurance
- Money supply
- Building permits

There are seven lagging indicators in the Conference Board Lagging Economic Index (LAG):

- Ratio of consumer installment credit to personal income
- Commercial and industrial loans outstanding
- Average duration of unemployment
- Change in labor cost per unit of output
- Change in prices (Consumer Price Index) for services
- Ratio of manufacturing to trade inventories
- Average prime rate charged by banks

So any economic measure must be either leading or lagging, right? No, nothing is ever quite so simple. Some indicators are considered to be right in the middle, or coincident indicators. The Conference Board tracks four of these in its Coincident Economic Index (CEI):

- Personal income minus transfer payments (like Social Security)
- Manufacturing and trade sales
- Nonagricultural employees on payrolls
- Industrial production

Why You Should Care

You may want to keep track of these indexes and the general movement of indicators, especially leading economic indicators. It is possible to track some of the leading indicators yourself, like the stock market and Consumer Confidence indexes, before seeing them compiled into this "big picture." Investors, in particular, find the LEI/CEI/LAG indexes to come late in the reporting cycle, too late to buy or sell on the news. But to get the big picture, and to understand the news as it comes at you, these measures can be helpful.

14. DISTRIBUTION OF INCOME AND WEALTH

If everything were perfect in today's economy, it would perform in line with a slogan rooted, ironically, in Socialist ideals: "From each according to his abilities; to each according to his needs." That is to say, in this perfect world, income and wealth distribution are natural and track economic contributions exactly. You work and you're paid the exact value of what you produce, and so is everyone else. You reap what you sow. You spend what you earn, or preferably a little less, as you save for the future. Your investments grow exactly in line with the economy. The economy grows, you grow, and everyone prospers.

Unfortunately, it doesn't work that way. While the United States and many Western economies are capitalistic and free and the so-called "invisible hand" doles out benefits largely commensurate with contributions, the largest income and greatest wealth don't always accrue to those who produce the most.

What You Should Know

Economists concern themselves with the inequality of income and wealth distribution. In terms of household income, the U.S. median in 2009 was $47,637, meaning that 50 percent of all households earned more, 50 percent earned less. The 20th percentile level was $20,453, while the 80th percentile and 95th percentile were $100,000 and $180,001 respectively. That's a large gap, and that gap has been growing in recent years. Between 1980 and 2009, the gain in income for the top 5 percent of Americans was 43 percent, or 4.3 times the 10 percent gain experienced by the lowest 20th percentile over the same period. Since the income base at the high levels is larger, the disproportionate size in percentage gains is even more significant. While some of this is explained by the growth in double-income households, one basic fact cannot be denied: the wealthy are getting wealthier, while the poor are getting poorer.

However, there is a difference between income and wealth.

In financial terms, wealth is the items of value a person owns, whereas income is the economic value a person receives as a result of work or investing, but does not necessarily retain. It's helpful to remember that income is a *cause*; wealth is an *effect*.

So some economists also focus on the distribution of wealth. As a matter of brevity, rather than sharing wealth statistics, I direct you to the fascinating study done by the U.S. Federal Reserve every three years known as the Survey of Consumer Finances. This survey not only points out the characteristics of wealth distribution and asset ownership, it also provides a fabulous benchmark for you to see where you stack up against other citizens. You can view the survey at *www.federalreserve.gov/pubs/oss/oss2/scfindex.html*.

Finally, it is sobering to examine worldwide data on this subject. According to statistics published by the United Nations University World Institute for Development Economics Research (UNU-WIDER) back in 2006 but still quite relevant:

- North America represents 5.2 percent of the world's population and 34.4 percent of the world's net worth
- Europe represents 9.6 percent of the population and 29.2 percent of the net worth
- Asia represents 52.2 percent of the population and 25.6 percent of the net worth
- Africa represents 10.7 percent of the population and 0.54 percent of the net worth

Why You Should Care

The distribution of wealth and income at a national level are interesting topics, especially for policymakers and social scientists. Efforts to redistribute wealth, for good or bad, become part of tax policy.

For individuals, it's important to know where you stand and to make sure your income—*cause*—is creating some wealth for you—*effect*. It's also important to make sure what you're calling "wealth" is truly wealth—not a fiction in a pretty wrapper known as the "wealth effect" (see #15 The Wealth Effect). Finally, it's good to appreciate the advantages you have compared to others in the United States and the world. As stressful and depressing as things seem at a given point in time, understanding income and wealth distribution on the U.S.

and worldwide stages will make you realize how much better off you really are.

15. THE WEALTH EFFECT

Have a lot of dough in the bank? Stocks been doing well? House has gone up (or recovered) $100,000 in value in the last two years? You might feel like spending money even if your income hasn't gone up a bit. Why? Because of the *wealth effect*.

What You Should Know

Wealth effects can happen when people actually *are* richer (when their incomes rise) or when people *feel* richer—as they did in a *big* way twice this past decade—because of the increase in the value of stocks, real estate, or other assets. The latter effect is dangerous because asset prices don't always match asset values, and things can change quickly.

The wealth effect created in the 2005–2007 real estate boom became doubly dangerous as people not only felt wealthier but used that wealth—their home values—to borrow money to buy things they couldn't otherwise afford. They used their homes as ATM machines. When prices came back to earth, not only were these unfortunate citizens less wealthy, they also had a lot of new debts to pay. The subsequent deleveraging (see #9 Deleveraging) caused a steep drop in economic activity and a vicious circle of unemployment, falling asset values, and still more unserviceable debt we all became familiar with.

Two scenarios can get people to spend more: (1) They are *actually* richer, be it through a raise, bonus, or some other form of increased income; (2) They *perceive* themselves to be richer, for example with an increase in their portfolio or assessed home value.

Interestingly, the wealth effect can turn on a dime. A January 2008 Gallup Poll reported that 56 percent of Americans thought their standard of living was getting better, while only 26 percent thought it was getting worse. By February 2009, those figures had reversed: 33 percent of Americans thought their standard of living was getting better while 44 percent thought it was getting worse. As we emerged from the Great Recession, people became once again more optimistic, and a resurgence in the stock markets has helped make people more comfortable with their finances—but it didn't cause a huge boom. As economist Robert Samuelson put it: "Careless optimism has given way to stubborn cautiousness."

Why You Should Care.

For starters, never equate the accumulation of "stuff" with being rich, and never count your asset chickens—particularly noncash assets—before they're hatched. You should never expand your lifestyle based on such asset values, but rather income and real worth after current and future obligations (like a college education or retirement) are met. Once people attain a standard of living they cannot afford, it is devilishly difficult to go back. The tendency is to expand further, borrow more, and become even more vulnerable.

Don't let the wealth effect make you overconfident, complacent, or even arrogant. When you feel you can afford anything without really running the numbers, that's either a sign that you're really rich or that you're a victim of the wealth effect. When that happens tap the brakes and retreat to the basic lifestyle truly congruent with your real income and wealth. Someday you'll be glad you did.

CHAPTER 3

Money, Prices, and Interest Rates

What would an economy be without money? For that matter, how would life work without money? Sure, you could exchange an hour on your job directly for a package of T-bone steaks, a sack of potatoes, and a bottle of wine, but how complicated would that be? Especially when your cube buddy wants the makings for a Caesar salad instead. And what would happen if you needed to go to the doctor, and all you had to pay with was your steak and potatoes?

Yes, money simplifies the economic picture by giving us a standard of exchange. Money is simply a commodity that can be universally exchanged as "legal tender" for all other commodities and services. It is the lifeblood of an economy. Yes, it *does* make the world go round.

Like any other commodity, there can be too much of it or too little, and its true worth is judged only by the value of other commodities. So like the economy it supports, the value and worth of money can change over time. Those changes become apparent as changes in *prices*. Furthermore, unlike most other commodities, money can be used as a lever or tool to moderate, manage, or control the economy. Economists and policymakers concern themselves with the worth of money, the cost of money, and the use of money to influence the economy. This chapter covers money and its interaction with the economy.

16. MONEY

You probably wouldn't be reading this book if you weren't interested in money—or at least, the necessities and pleasures that money buys.

What You Should Know

Technically speaking, money is anything that is generally accepted as payment for goods and services and repayment of debts. Usually, it comes in the form of paper or coins, but anything could be used as tender, even bottle caps, if society set an accepted standard for using bottle caps as payment. Money is used primarily as a medium of exchange, but also as a unit of measure of financial activity and as a store of value.

As a medium of exchange, money works because of its universal acceptance. If you try to pay for a cartful of groceries with a goat, it might work, but only if the grocer happens to need or want a goat. Money is designed to work for everybody, no matter what they need or want to purchase. It is much more efficient than direct barter. Although "plastic"—credit and debit cards—has seemingly replaced money, it isn't really money, only a convenient way to administer the payment; the real money changes hands later on behind the scenes.

As a unit of measure, or "unit of account," as economists call it, money is a handy means to place a value on things. A tab for $104 worth of groceries is much easier to comprehend than a tab for 2⅔ goats. Likewise, imagine the difficulties measuring GDP, incomes, and so forth without money. Finally, money is divisible into known and like units; if one were trading in diamonds instead, no two diamonds are worth the exact same amount, and would thus complicate the exchange.

The money we see comes in the form of currency—that is, printed paper and minted coinage representing units of generally accepted value. As a store of value, one can convert anything to money, at least for the short term, and store the value there until something else is purchased. Many economists caution against relying on money as a store of value for too long, as the increase in money supply (see #17 Money Supply) over time makes a unit of money worth relatively less. Some question whether current economic policies in the United States, Japan, and other countries will drive the value of money down and threaten its status as a store of value.

The vast majority of money doesn't exist as $20, $10, $5, and $1 bills, but rather as deposits in banks. Those sums of money—and almost everyone has some—can be created by credit and moved around with a check (the old way) or the click of a mouse or keyboard.

Finally, U.S. money is a type of money known as *fiat* money, meaning that its value, and that it be accepted as a means of payment, is determined by government order. It is not backed by any hard asset such as gold. Technically, you can only exchange a U.S. dollar with the U.S. government for another dollar. Until the 1960s, that wasn't true—you could exchange currency for gold or silver, depending on the type of money you held.

Why You Should Care

It's always useful to step back and think about what money really is. It isn't an end in and of itself; it is a unit of exchange. It can be exchanged for something else later on. Understanding what money *is* and what it's *for* can give you a more balanced perspective for managing your finances.

17. MONEY SUPPLY

Money is a commodity, just like any other commodity you might purchase with it. The money supply is the amount of money within an economy available for purchasing goods or services. The central banks—in the United States, the Federal Reserve— keep close tabs on the money supply, as the amount of money in circulation can have a big effect on the economy (see #30 Federal Reserve, #29 Central Bank, and #18 Inflation).

What You Should Know

Money is created by either printing paper tender or by making it available as credit through lending. When the central bank lowers interest rates, it stimulates the creation of more money through lending. When there is more money in circulation, people have more money and spend more money, stimulating demand for goods and services. That helps businesses and creates a stronger economy, but also threatens inflation, since more money is chasing the same amount of goods and services, making the money worth relatively less.

The Federal Reserve measures several categories of money supply, four of which are more mainstream and likely to be in the news. The M0 figure is so-called base money—currency (bills

M-0   currency, coins, central bank deposits
M-1   + demand deposits — 'most spendable' money
M-2   + savings accts, CDs
M-3   time deposits

and coins) and central bank deposits. The M1 figure includes so-called *demand deposits*, roughly equivalent to amounts in checking accounts—money on hand as a deposit in an institution designed to be used actively to buy and sell goods and services in the short term. The M1 is the most "spendable" money in circulation at a given point in time. The M2 adds money in time deposits like savings accounts and CDs—money that is there but not as likely to be used actively for transactions. And M3 adds large time deposits like repurchase agreements and institutional money market accounts—also long-term in nature, and largely out of consumer hands. Economists tie their horse to M1 in terms of measuring the amount of money really flowing around and through the economy; it is like "working capital" in a business.

Why You Should Care

Bernanke, 2012, 13, 14

Economists watch money supply to forecast inflation and other economic effects. If you see reports of increasing money supply, it can mean good times ahead, but it can also mean inflation. Be suspicious of prolonged money supply increases—the government and particularly the Fed may be sacrificing the future by driving down the value of money in an attempt to realize a short-term gain in business activity and employment.

18. INFLATION

Inflation is an across-the-board rise in prices of goods and services over a period of time. When inflation is present, the purchasing power of a given unit of money buys fewer goods and services; that is, the "real" value of money is less. The idea of inflation is generally scary, as nobody wants to see the decline in the value of money. But if kept in check, some inflation is actually okay, and may even be beneficial.

What You Should Know

Inflation is generally measured by two indexes tracked as "basket of goods" proxies of overall price activity, the Consumer Price Index (CPI) and the Producer Price Index (PPI). The Department of Labor's Bureau of Labor Statistics publishes both figures, along with a *core* CPI figure that strips out the "more volatile" food and energy components. Since we all need food and energy, some choose to ignore the "core" figure.

Inflation can be caused by changes in demand, supply, or a combination of the two. Demand-based, or *demand-pull*, inflation occurs when people have too much money or too much cheap money (that is, easy credit), and it chases a fixed level of goods and services. The antidote is to make money more expensive by raising interest rates or decreasing the amount of money available, both normally well in the control of the central bank, in our case the Federal Reserve. Inflation can also be caused by shortages of a commodity, like oil, where price spikes will eventually trickle into the entire economy. Or they can be a combination of the two, as seen in early 2008 when both a supply shortage and a demand increase driven mostly by China drove energy prices higher with a fairly rapid trickling through the economy.

Depending on the amount and consistency of inflation, it can have positive or negative effects on the economy. Too much inflation discourages saving, as the purchasing power of that saving will deteriorate. High inflation may create shortages as people "stock up" in anticipation of rising prices. It creates fear and uncertainty in the business world, delaying business investment, because no one can predict what raw materials, labor, and other "inputs" will cost in the future.

Modest inflation—in the 2 to 4 percent per-year range—is seen as a good thing. Why? Because it's better than the opposite: deflation (see #19 Deflation). Moderate and predictable inflation is thought to help avoid recessions and sharper business cycle reversals. Inflation also helps borrowers, for the dollars they will use to pay back debts will be worth less in the future, thus easier to come by, as most debts do not get larger with inflation.

It's interesting to note that inflation and deflation once occurred in sharp and unpredictable cycles. More recently, central bank intervention has moderated those cycles, and has avoided deflation altogether, at least in the United States, since the Great Depression. The moderate and steady inflation rates enjoyed particularly since the oil shocks of the 1970s have created a favorable business climate. See Figure 3.1 for a long history of inflation rates. (It should be noted that this chart is the same as presented in the first edition and only takes us through 2006, but the 356 years before that remain instructive)

Figure 3.1 U.S. Historical Inflation Rate

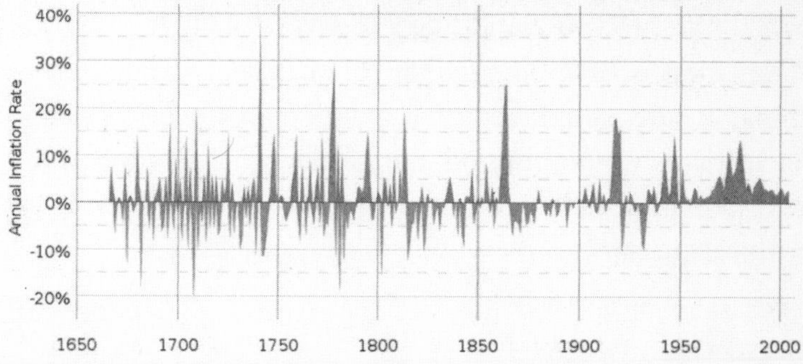

Source: Wikipedia

Data Source: John J. McCusker, *How Much Is That in Real Money?: A Historical Commodity Price Index for Use as a Deflator of Money Values in the Economy of the United States*, American Antiquarian Society, 2001; Consumer Price Index (from 2001 forward)

Why You Should Care

Inflation can be one of the biggest enemies to your finances and financial plans, particularly if you save money. Those savings will be worth less over time if the rate of inflation exceeds the interest rate your savings earn. Most recently, wage increases have not kept up with inflation, another cause for concern. Hard assets like gold and real estate are thought to hold up better in inflationary times, but obviously real estate is no longer as safe a haven as once thought. These days, people have learned to fight inflation by consuming less or buying less expensive goods and services, but that isn't a strategy for the long term. Inflation remains a persistent threat to finances for all of us, especially as central banks "fix" economic problems by increasing credit and the money supply. Although inflation hasn't been a big news headline lately, it's important to watch inflation closely—particularly in the things you tend buy a lot of, including food, health care, and energy.

19. DEFLATION

If inflation is bad, doesn't that mean that deflation is a good thing? It sure would seem that a decline in the prices of goods and services would be good; our money would be worth more, and we'd all be able to buy more for our money. What's wrong with *this* picture?

What You Should Know

Actually, economists hate deflation, which is defined as a sustained, across-the-board *decrease* in prices, a *negative* inflation rate. Why? Because, quite simply, if people perceive that prices will go down, they'll stop spending and wait for those prices to go down further. Businesses will do the same thing. Furthermore, businesses won't be able to sell their products for as much money in the future, and are using relatively more expensively priced materials and labor they have to buy today to produce them in advance of that sale. So for the business, profits suffer; for everybody, the slowdown caused by people hoarding money anticipating it will become worth more later ends up sapping the economy.

Reduced consumer and business spending can cause a severe business slump; in fact, deflation is typically only observed during the most severe business crises, including the Great Depression and the so-called "lost decade" in Japan that started in the 1990s. In Japan, a large inflationary bubble driven by real estate and irresponsible lending unwound. Prices started to drop and banks stopped lending, starting a downward spiral of decreased consumption and spending that didn't let up until recently, when the central Bank of Japan took rather drastic measures—that is, printing lots of money—to artificially decrease the value of the yen and rekindle mild inflation.

The good news is that we haven't really seen deflation lately, although there was a persistent threat of it as a consequence of the Great Recession. Figure 3.1 illustrates the fact that deflation occurred considerably more often in the past.

Why You Should Care

For most individuals, deflation isn't that scary, unless it is prolonged and leads to an extended business slump. That, of course, means a more severe contraction of business, and additional job losses. The bigger problem can be the actions of central banks like the Fed, which go so far to *avoid* deflation, they end up sowing seeds of a stronger *inflation*. That was the big worry in the wake of the Great Recession. Bottom line: the less you hear about deflation, the better.

20. STAGFLATION

As the name implies, stagflation is a painful combination of inflation and economic malaise. Since the "typical" cause of inflation is excessive demand in an overheated economy, the combination is a bit surprising for economic purists. But the occurrence of both together happened in a big way in the late 1970s, when high inflation was accompanied by high unemployment, and it continues to be a threat to the current economy both in the United States and abroad (see #10 Misery Index).

What You Should Know

Stagflation generally has two causes. One is a supply shock, as in the oil shocks in the late 1970s, and to a degree, the oil price spike in 2008. Inflation is caused more by supply factors than general demand, and so the traditional means of fighting inflation through monetary policy (reducing money supply, raising interest rates) don't work—they only serve to slow the economy while not solving the supply shortage. Stagflation can also be caused by excessive regulation, or by other practices that make economies inefficient, combined with inflationary monetary policy. Such has been the case in Europe and Latin America from time to time.

Why You Should Care

For the U.S. consumer, the sort of stagflation caused by oil shocks or similar shortages creates the most concern. If you see inflation in the economy, particularly energy and food prices, that should not be taken as signs of a robust economy; more likely, the economy will sink as higher prices sap the strength, like a tax, of the economy. If the government tries to deal with these effects by tightening the money supply, look out—especially if you're in an economically sensitive vocation.

The good news: the sort of stagflation caused by regulation or economic inefficiencies is less likely to happen in the United States than elsewhere. Despite what it may seem like sometimes, the U.S. economy is considered to have one of the easiest and most consistent regulatory climates of any developed country. This is why many economists are concerned when they hear cries for more regulation, and why they became concerned with some of the proposed policy changes that came with the recent economic crisis—they want to preserve the "stable state" the United States offers for capitalist commerce.

21. INTEREST RATES

An *interest rate* is the price a borrower pays to borrow money. The key word is *price*—for whatever reason, possibly owing to the negative references to the borrowing and lending of money in the Bible, the concept that interest is a price paid for the use of something, in this case, money, is poorly understood by most. If you think of interest rates as a price, sometimes too high, sometimes a bargain, you'll learn to make better decisions when evaluating a borrowing opportunity.

From your point of view, interest rates are a price, or cost, of using money. They are also the price, or benefit received, for letting someone else use *your* money, as in when you deposit money in a bank or buy a bond. Finally, on a national scale, interest rates are also a vital tool used by governments to control money supply and the availability of credit, and thus to exert some control over the economy.

What You Should Know

Interest rates are normally expressed as a percentage of a borrowed balance over the period of one year. Many interest rates are quoted as a nominal, or ongoing, interest rate, with an "annualized percentage rate" quoted in parallel to account for *all* borrowing costs, including fees, associated with a borrowing transaction, on an annual basis. Federal law requires publication of APRs to allow simple "apples-to-apples" comparisons of the price to borrow money.

The interest rate, or price, for the use of borrowed funds depends on several factors:

1. **Length of loan term.** How long will you keep the money you borrow? That will influence the price, because of two things. First is the opportunity foregone by the owner of the money to spend it or invest it in something else. People tend to prefer *liquidity*—that is, to have their money available to spend. Second is the risk of default or inflation, which increases the longer you hold the money. Under normal circumstances, the longer you hold the money, the more you will pay for it, and if it's your money, the longer you lend it, the more you can collect.

2. **Inflationary expectations.** When inflation is high—that is, money is losing value fast—you'll be able to pay back with cheaper, more plentiful dollars later. As a result, high inflationary expectations usually lead to higher *nominal*, or quoted, interest rates, although the *real* interest rate (interest rate minus inflation rate) may stay the same.

3. **Risk.** In any lending situation, there's always the risk that the borrower will go bankrupt or not be able to pay back for some other reason. As a result, lenders assess this risk, sometimes very methodically, and may charge a risk

premium (see #24 Risk Premium), or an interest rate above the going market rate, to account for this risk. A company or government entity with a poor credit rating, likewise, will be forced to pay higher rates.

4. **Taxes.** The interest paid by municipalities and certain other public entities is nontaxable, so these entities can pay a lower interest rate and the recipients still come out the same, since they don't have to pay taxes on the income. As a result, tax-free bond interest rates can be 20 to 40 percent lower than taxable interest rates.

There are literally hundreds of different interest rates in the marketplace for different kinds of loans or securities of different term lengths, risk factors, and tax status. For most people, the following are most important:

BORROWING RATES
- Fed funds rate (see #31 Target Interest Rates) as a leading indicator of other rates and general Fed economic policy
- Prime rate (see #22 Prime Rate), another barometer of market interest rates
- 30-year mortgage rate
- Credit card interest rates—not because they change but because they can be very costly, as much as 25 percent above "market" interest rates. That's an expensive price premium.

SAVINGS RATES
- Certificate of Deposit (CD) rates, an important form of savings
- Money market rates (see #76 Money Market Fund)

Why You Should Care

Interest rates affect all of us directly or indirectly. Directly, they determine how much we pay to borrow money for homes, cars, education, and so forth, and they determine how much income we receive on savings—which has been a big issue for many lately who depend on interest income, especially to fund retirement. Indirectly, interest rates and *changes* in interest rates can give strong clues to which way the economy is going, and which way policymakers *want* it to go.

22. PRIME RATE

Not too many years ago, news headlines featured any change in the so-called prime rate. Whenever it changed in one direction or the other, it was considered news. Although it has declined in importance, the prime rate is still used as a benchmark or reference interest rate by banks, economists, and others in the business world.

What You Should Know

The prime rate, or "prime lending rate," is, in theory, the interest rate banks charged their best, lowest-risk customers. The loans in question were largely unsecured and short term, so the prime rate was a representation of how much the credit was really worth in the marketplace. These days the prime rate is more likely tied to Treasury security rates or to "average cost of funds" figures published by the government; some interest rates are quoted as a percentage above or below the prime rate.

In the United States, the prime rate has typically run 3 percentage points, or 300 *basis points* for those of you wishing to sound financially sophisticated, above the target federal funds rate set by the Fed.

Why You Should Care

Most people don't care as much about prime rates as they did ten to twenty years ago, although they are still used as a benchmark for change. Today, the Fed funds rate, Treasury bill and bond rates, and mortgage rates are more broadly accepted measures of interest rates and interest rate direction.

23. YIELD CURVE

Economists and others in the financial community use the yield curve to plot the relationship between yield, or interest rate return, and maturity, or length of time a debt security is held. The most frequently reported yield curve compares the three-month, two-year, five-year, and thirty-year U.S. Treasury debt.

Generally speaking, the longer a debt security is held, the higher the interest rate. That's because of the greater opportunity costs and the greater risks, including inflation, over the longer time period (see #21 Interest Rates). But depending on economic circumstances and central bank policy, the relationship between yield and maturity can change or even reverse. So economists watch yield curves closely for signs of economic health, and financial professionals watch the curve for signs of preference for different kinds of debt securities, such as mortgage rates or bank lending rates.

What You Should Know

The normal yield curve (Figure 3.2) shows rates gradually rising as maturity lengthens. This curve can be steeper if investors see more risk in longer-term securities, typically in inflationary times or times where other risk factors like corporate defaults come to the forefront. The yield curve typically flattens (Figure 3.3) when the Federal Reserve raises short-term interest rates to slow the economy, and can even go to an "inverted" state (Figure 3.4), where short-term yields exceed long-term yields, if the Fed acts strongly to restrict money supply. Economists see an inverted yield curve as a sign of a looming recession if the economy cools, as the Fed apparently desires.

Figure 3.2 Normal Yield Curve

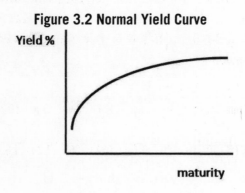

Figure 3.3 Flat Yield Curve

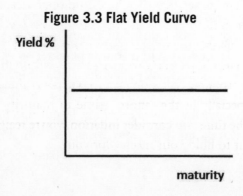

Figure 3.4 Inverted Yield Curve

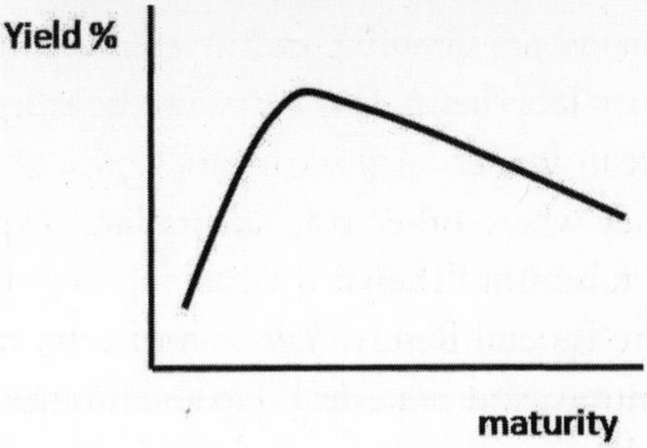

You can watch the yield curve by observing short- and long-term Treasury security and other rates in the financial section of a newspaper or websites. The U.S. Treasury publishes yield curve data (not a chart, unfortunately) at *www.ustreas.gov/offices/domestic-finance/debt-management/interest-rate/yield.shtml*.

On July 1, 2013, the following rates were posted on this Treasury webpage:

Time to Maturity	1 mo	2 mo	6 mo	1 yr	2 yr	3 yr	5 yr	10 yr	20 yr	30 yr
Treasury Yield	0.01%	0.04	0.09	0.15	.034	.065	1.39	1.93	3.19	3.48

It's not hard to see that these rates, although ticked up slightly from earlier in the year, are still historically low. It's also not hard to see that for income-oriented investors, this is a grim story—while if you're a borrower, this is attractive, although since you're not the government, you don't get to borrow at these exact rates. In fact, especially at the "short" (time to maturity) end of the curve, by the time you consider inflation, you're really paying the government to hold your money for you.

If you're an active income-dependent investor, you'll want to watch these numbers carefully, and if you're a numbers kind of person in general, it's interesting to watch these figures fluctuate.

Why You Should Care

Aside from the economic signals it sends, the yield curve also helps you figure out the best "deal" for your money as a depositor or borrower. If the yield curve is relatively flat or inverted, it is best to look for shorter-term CDs or other time deposits; likewise, it's a better time to look for a longer-term, say a thirty-year, mortgage. If the curve is normal and steep, a thirty-year mortgage will cost significantly more, and you'll do better if you can stretch your payment into a twenty-, fifteen- or ten-year mortgage. As an investor, you should seek longer-term savings deposits or bonds.

24. RISK PREMIUM

In economics and finance, the "risk premium" is the expected additional return on an investment to compensate for the risk of that type of investment. It is the difference between the actual return rate and a "risk-free" return rate often represented by Treasury securities or some other risk-free standard.

In finance, the risk premium can be the expected rate of return above the risk-free interest rate. When measuring risk, a common-sense approach is to compare the risk-free return on T-bills and the very risky return on other investments. The difference between these two returns can be interpreted as a measure of the excess return on the average risky asset. This excess return is known as the risk premium.

What You Should Know

The explanation of risk premiums can get fairly technical, so the best way to describe them is by example. Suppose you're considering buying a ten-year corporate bond that pays 4 percent. If a ten-year Treasury bond is currently paying 2 percent (see #23 Yield Curve), then you would be receiving a additional 2 percent to cover the risk of the company's credit quality, or default. Similarly, if you buy a stock expecting a 5 percent or greater return on it, the difference between that return and 2 percent would be your expectation to compensate you for the risk.

Part of the reason the normal yield curve (see #23 Yield Curve) slopes upward as maturity lengthens is to cover the additional risk inherent in longer maturities. That risk can come from *default risk*, *interest rate risk* (the risk that interest rates might rise over the holding period), and *inflation risk*. All three of these types of risk are built into a risk premium. The risk premium also takes into account any collateral pledged on the loan and the "seniority"—that is, the order in which any debt would be paid in a bankruptcy or liquidation.

Why You Should Care

Unless you're employed in the world of high finance, you probably won't encounter the term "risk premium" very often in your work, or even in your investing. It's best to think about it conceptually. When you make an investment, you should ask yourself: "Does the expected return on this investment compensate me for the risk I'm taking?" If it does, the risk premium is in line with reality, and the investment may make sense. If the risk premium is insufficient—that is, the payoff doesn't compensate you for the risk compared to a risk-free return—look elsewhere.

25. BOND PRICES VERSUS INTEREST RATES

> "Bonds were up today. The ten-year Treasury
> was up 23/32 in active trading."

You hear it on the news. But what does it mean when bond prices go up? Is that a good thing, like hearing about stock prices going up?

The answer is—it depends. Yes, the above news item is usually good news. It's obviously good news if you already own bonds— your bonds went up in value. But it's also good news if you're planning to borrow money, because it means market interest rates are lower.

What You Should Know

When a bond price goes up, that means market interest rates have moved lower. Why? Because bonds are sold originally with a fixed *coupon,* or interest payment. A bond issued and sold at a typical $1,000 face value that yields 4 percent will pay exactly $40 per year in interest, period. It may pay that interest once a year, or in two semiannual payments of $20—that doesn't really matter.

Even though most bonds are issued in $1,000 increments, they're quoted as if they sell for $100, a figure known as *par.* If that bond rises 23/32 (of a dollar), that's the equivalent of saying the bond price rose 71.9 cents to $100.72. Returning to the $1,000 face-value scenario, if you take the $40 in interest and divide it by $1007.20, you'll get an implied interest rate of 3.97 percent, down from the 4 percent it was originally sold for.

Here's the "it depends" part of bond prices and interest rates. Normally, the rise in bond prices and the corresponding fall in interest rates are a good thing. But first, that's only true if you're a borrower—if you're a saver, you prefer higher interest rates. Second, the rise in bond prices can often occur as a "flight to quality"—when other assets such as stocks are perceived as more risky, and investors flock to bonds. This may push interest rates down, but only at the expense of other economic pain.

Why You Should Care

So if you hear that bond prices rose, that means interest rates—rates you would receive or rates you would pay, say, on a mortgage or car loan—are going down. Conversely, if bond prices fall, that means that interest rates are going up. Especially if you're in the market for a mortgage, you want to watch the ups and downs of the bond market closely.

26. GOLD STANDARD

Are your dollars as good as gold? That's the central question to understanding what a gold standard is and how it works.

What You Should Know

In the gold standard monetary system, paper currency is pegged and convertible into preset, fixed quantities of gold. The supply of money is specifically tied to gold reserves held by central banks (see #16 Money and #17 Money Supply). The gold standard prevailed during the late 1800s and the first half of the twentieth century, but gradually subsided starting in the Great Depression, and was done away with altogether in 1971, after many years where $35 in paper could be exchanged for an ounce of actual gold. This means that central banks, including the Federal Reserve, effectively have no constraints in terms of expanding and contracting the money supply to affect monetary policy (see #56 Monetary Policy).

The gold standard was designed to protect a nation from abuses of monetary policy, and specifically the risk of hyperinflation from an overexpansion in the money supply. Today, we trust governments and central banks not to get carried away with monetary policy. Since no country actively uses the gold standard, those living in fear of hyperinflation buy the metal outright, and have pushed the price of gold up to a recent high of more than $1,900 an ounce, although it has subsided to the $1,200–$1,400 range recently—still high by historical standards.

Many economists following a traditional, pure capitalist, laissez-faire, government-can-do-more-harm-than-good doctrine favor a return to the gold standard (see #59 Austrian School). Doing so would be difficult and painful now, as the rate of currency growth has far outpaced the rate of gold production from mining. A return to the standard would entail a drastic reduction in the value of the dollar and most other currencies, as there wouldn't be enough gold to go around to back all of the dollars and other paper currencies in circulation.

Why You Should Care

The gold standard debate is theoretical for most of us, but serves as a reminder that money is simply a commodity, and if there is too much of it, its value goes down. Many investment advisers recommend holding at least some gold in your portfolio, as the actual metal or as commodity futures or gold mining stocks, to anchor at least a portion of your wealth to a gold standard. That's up to you—and there are plenty of downsides—but understanding the gold standard can help you think through such an investment.

CHAPTER 4

Banks and Central Banking

We have discussed the economy and money; the next logical thing to talk about is banks and the banking system. As grain elevators distribute grain and lumberyards distribute lumber, banks distribute money. They store your spare money and allocate it as capital to others (hopefully) who need it for a good economic reason.

Banks are part of a banking system and, for better or for worse, are interconnected. They are also moderated by a central banking authority, which in the United States is the Federal Reserve. This chapter describes the different kinds of banks, the banking system, the Federal Reserve, and some of the ways we measure bank strength and success.

27. COMMERCIAL BANK

For the most part, when you think of "bank," you're thinking of a commercial bank. A commercial bank serves the public—ordinary consumers and "main street" businesses—with an assortment of accounts, savings, checking, and loan services.

What You Should Know

A commercial bank gets funds from customer deposits, including checking and savings accounts, certificates of deposits (CDs), and other time deposits. It may also get funds by selling securities, especially government bonds back to the government, or by short-term borrowings from government or private investors. In turn, it earns income by lending those funds to businesses needing operating capital, and to consumers for a variety of purposes.

While they lend funds for businesses to use, commercial banks are distinguished from investment banks (see #28 Investment Bank) because they do not buy or sell securities for their own part or on behalf of individuals or corporate clients. In fact, huge bank losses on investments prior to the Great Depression led to the failure of many banks (some 20 percent of all banks failed), which then led to legislation, specifically the Glass-Steagall Act of 1933, prohibiting commercial banks from engaging in investment banking activities. That law was repealed in 1999, allowing megabanks like Citigroup and JPMorgan Chase to combine commercial, investment, and many other financial operations into a single holding company.

Arguably, that led to some of the problems seen in the recent global crisis, as the investment banking arms of several big banks put their entire company in jeopardy. The phrase "too big to fail" became part of the common citizen's vocabulary. Recently, the so-called "Volcker Rule" has reintroduced a ban, with certain exceptions, on commercial banks and their affiliates to engage in "proprietary trading"—that is, trading the markets for their own benefit using what amounts to your funds—but a full-scale reenactment of Glass-Steagall separation of commercial and investment banking activities hasn't happened. Although much is beyond the scope of our discussion, suffice it to say that commercial and investment banks are subject to different banking laws and capitalization rules.

It should also be noted that at one time there were significant differences between banks and so-called savings and loan, or "thrift," institutions. Many thrifts were nonprofit, and had regulatory restrictions on the source of their funds and the amount of interest they had to pay on funds acquired. A combination of regulation and poorly thought-out deregulation led to the S&L crisis in the late 1980s. Today, thrifts continue to exist, but are much more like commercial banks than in the early years. Most do not offer the complete array of services that commercial banks do, which now offer investments, business lending and advice, and general financial advice.

Why You Should Care

The banks you generally deal with are commercial banks, unless you're involved in securities trading, mergers and acquisitions, or in taking companies "public" by selling stock or other securities. Commercial banks are set up to handle your normal banking needs, and are regulated to provide the sort of banking products and safety (insured deposits, for example) that the general public expects.

28. INVESTMENT BANK

Never seen a local branch of Lehman Brothers? Or a Bear Stearns or Goldman Sachs ATM machine? There's a reason for that. The reason—although not as distinct as it once was—is that these big banking names are *investment banks*, not commercial banks (see #27 Commercial Bank). These banks are primarily in the securities business, not the general banking business.

What You Should Know

Investment banks are in business primarily to raise capital on behalf of clients, to advise them on mergers and other corporate restructuring, and to make markets for securities. Clients include corporations, governments, pension funds, and large investment companies like mutual funds. In fact, they not only buy and sell securities on behalf of clients, but they also try to make money by dealing in the markets on their own behalf, in an activity known as *proprietary trading*. While this is once again illegal for commercial banks because of the recently enacted "Volcker Rule" (see #27 Commercial Bank and #39 Dodd-Frank), it is still a big part of what investment banks do.

Investment banks assist a company in selling new shares of stock, or bonds, or other securities to raise capital. For corporations, they will advise on mergers, acquisitions, and divestitures, and then do the financial legwork to execute these transactions. As securities dealers, most investment banks act as dealer, buying and selling shares in the open market on their own behalf or on behalf of clients.

The days of separate and individual investment banks are almost over with the 2008 demise of Bear Stearns and Lehman Brothers, two of the last independent investment banks. Most have been combined into larger holding companies as an arm of a larger, combined commercial/investment banking company, like Credit Suisse or Barclays. These so-called "universal banks" took center stage in the 2008 banking crisis, although in the case of JPMorgan Chase and others, well-managed banking diversification has proven beneficial.

Why You Should Care

You will generally not run into investment banks, or the investment-banking arm of larger universal banks, in your ordinary business. Investment banks have traditionally made huge amounts of money facilitating transactions (a quarter or a half percent "crumb" off of a billion-dollar transaction is still a lot of money). It remains to be seen what the future of investment banking is to become, and how much the regulatory environment will change. For most consumers, it may prove to have little effect.

29. CENTRAL BANK

As the name implies, a "central bank" is central to the banking and monetary system of a nation. The central bank plays several key roles in the economy, including setting and carrying out monetary policy, maintaining the stability of the nation's currency, and supporting and regulating individual banks and the banking system. The Federal Reserve (see #30 Federal Reserve) functions as the central bank in the United States, while the European Central Bank (ECB) is the central bank for the sixteen member states of the so-called Eurozone. Other central banks include the Bank of Japan, the People's Bank of China, and the Bank of England.

What You Should Know

Central banks control money supply and currency stability through monetary policy (see #56 Monetary Policy). That is done by setting target interest rates (see #31 Target Interest Rates) and more directly through open market operations (see #32 Fed Open Market Operations), where they buy and sell government bonds to inject cash into or remove it from the economy. Central banks also control the amount of currency—paper and coin—in the economy.

Central banks lend money to other banks when needed, and act as a "lender of last resort" during financial crises. The financial crisis that triggered the Great Recession saw the Federal Reserve, in coordination with the U.S. Treasury, take a more activist role in propping up not only banks but also other players in the economy. While the "propping up" scenario is largely past, today's Fed continues to boost the economy through open market operations—still in mid-2013 buying about $85 billion in bonds every month to infuse more cash into the economy through its "quantitative easing" programs—so-called "QE3" and "QE4." Central banks may make these operations "public," declaring them in the media and in their own published minutes to achieve maximum economic effect (in the most recent case, optimism)—and they may also conduct open market operations "under the radar" so as not to affect or disturb the markets. The Fed and other central banks may also project and communicate future activities, as seen with the so-called "tapering" of bond purchases widely prognosticated, also in mid-2013.

Central banks also set and enforce important banking and finance ground rules. These rules and requirements include governing how much capital banks must keep in reserve (see #36 Reserve Requirements), and how much equity stock investors must have in a stock transaction involving borrowing, or *margin* (see #86 Margin and Buying on Margin). In some countries, like China, central banks actively manage the country's foreign currency exchange and exchange rates.

Notably, most central banks operate somewhat independently of the nation's political authority to avoid political gridlock and to be able to do what's best for the economy on short notice. The U.S. Federal Reserve can create money "with the stroke of a keyboard" without Congressional approval.

Why You Should Care

The health and welfare of any economy is carefully monitored and controlled by a country's central bank. Observing the central bank's actions will give you a forward look into what's ahead for the economy. If the central bank is raising target interest rates, for instance, a slowdown is intended and likely on the horizon. If the central bank is lowering interest rates and injecting money into the system, that signals that the slowdown is at hand and the central bank is acting to reverse a slumping economy. It is also worth listening to comments made by the leaders of the central banks—Ben Bernanke (soon to be Janet Yellen) of the U.S. Federal Reserve and Jean-Claude Trichet of the ECB—for signs of economic health or concern.

30. FEDERAL RESERVE

The Federal Reserve functions as the U.S. central bank. The Federal Reserve System was created by the Federal Reserve Act of 1913 in response to the Panic of 1907, earlier panics in 1873 and 1893, and an accepted need for a stronger central banking system. Known simply as "the Fed," the Federal Reserve carries out a broad range of activities to ensure the stability and prosperity of the U.S. economy.

What You Should Know

The Federal Reserve is not a single bank or institution but rather a system of committees, advisory councils, and twelve member banks located through the United States. The details of this structure aren't important, but you'll hear about the Board of Governors, of which Ben Bernanke was the chair through

FOMC

February 2014, and the twelve-member Open Market Committee (FOMC), which meets eight times a year and makes policy decisions affecting target interest rates and ultimately, money supply (see #31 Target Interest Rates, #17 Money Supply, and #56 Monetary Policy).

The Federal Reserve was created to address banking panics, but in the modern era has taken on a more active role in managing and moderating the economy. Most visible is the management of money supply through monetary policy, toward the stated and often conflicting goals of maximum employment and stable prices (translation: avoidance of inflation and deflation). The Fed regulates banking and banking institutions and other credit instruments, including the credit rights of consumers. Credit protection regulations are created and enforced by the Fed through laws passed by Congress, including the Truth in Lending, Equal Credit Opportunity, and Home Mortgage Disclosure acts (see #48 Credit Protection). The Fed manages the relationships between the banks and government, banks and consumers, and banks with each other.

The Fed has roles beyond managing the banking system and money supply too numerous to recount here. Among those goals are managing financial stability in times of crisis and improving the financial standing of the United States in the world economy. The Fed played a very active role in preventing systemic meltdown in the 2008–2009 financial crisis, acting as "lender of last resort" in addition to its traditional role in providing financial stimulus. The Fed announced several new programs, or lending "facilities," like the so-called "TARP," or Troubled Asset Relief Program, to help banks and other businesses get short-term credit; some of these programs hadn't been seen since the Great Depression.

Critics contend that the Fed may be playing *too* active a role in managing the economy; in its zeal to create stability and manage the business cycle, it is making us as a nation more vulnerable to unintended consequences that may have far-reaching and much more serious effects. Through monetary policy and the new lending facilities, the Fed injected huge and unprecedented amounts of money into the economy; many worry about the long-term inflationary effects of this massive injection (see #34 Reflation).

Why You Should Care

What happens in the U.S. economy has always been influenced and to a degree controlled by the Fed. Most recently, the Fed, by necessity and somewhat by choice, has become much more involved in trying to manage and stabilize economic outcomes. You should watch what the Fed says and does, and think through the long-term consequences of its economic policies and actions. It's also worth understanding the credit and banking protections the Fed has put in place.

31. TARGET INTEREST RATES

Central to the task of the Federal Reserve and other central banks is to manage the nation's money supply and to stimulate or slow down economic activity to stabilize prices, maintain employment, and foster moderate economic growth. Central banks use target interest rates as well as direct injections of money into the financial system to moderate interest rates and to accomplish these other economic goals.

Interest rates work like a brake or accelerator on an economy. Lower rates make money "cheaper"—that is, cheaper to borrow, and thus more available for economic activity. Conversely, higher interest rates make money more expensive, thus acting as a brake on the economy, which ultimately helps to control inflation.

What You Should Know

Every economy has target interest rates managed through central bank policy. In the United States, the Fed controls the *discount rate* directly, and manages the *federal funds rate*, or "Fed funds rate," through open market operations (see #32 Fed Open Market Operations). In Europe, the LIBOR, or London Interbank Offered Rate, is the primary target interest rate.

The Fed funds rate is more important—and more complicated —than the discount rate, and is a key component of monetary policy. Specifically, it's the rate that banks charge each other for overnight loans of reserves they hold at the Fed. The Fed does not actually set this rate, but rather influences and controls it by changing the money supply through open market operations. When the Federal Open Market Committee meets, as it does eight times a year, it sets the target for the Fed funds rate, leaving it unchanged, or raising or lowering it, usually in increments of 0.25 or 0.50 percent. Open market operations do the rest. The Fed funds rate is the most important and most closely watched tool in the Fed's policy arsenal, and it becomes the base for many other interest rates throughout the economy, including the prime rate (see #22 Prime Rate), which is typically about 3 percent above the Fed funds rate.

In the Great Recession and its aftermath the Fed was so concerned about propping up the economy that it lowered the Fed funds rate to an unprecedented 0.25 percent, and it has ranged between 0 and 0.25 percent ever since. To put that into context, it's interesting to look at the Fed funds rate over the last fifty-five years:

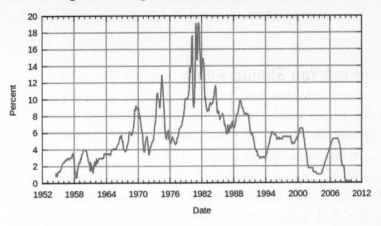

Figure 4.1 Target Fed Funds Rate, 1954–2009

Source: The Federal Reserve

Figure 4.1 shows pronounced swings in the rate, including a drastic and—in hindsight—somewhat misguided spike in the rate in the early 1980s to mitigate an inflationary spiral that was as much caused by supply constraints (oil) as overheated demand. You can also see the swings over the last twenty-five years as the Fed has tried, with some success, to moderate the business cycle. Finally, although the chart itself has only been updated through 2009, there's been little reason to update it since, because the effective rate continues to hover near zero.

The *discount rate* is the rate at which the Fed will lend funds directly to member banks. The Fed sets this rate directly, but sets it usually a percent or so higher than the Fed funds rate to encourage banks to lend to each other instead of borrowing from the Fed.

To understand global credit conditions and interest rates, many now refer to LIBOR, or London Interbank Offered Rate—a composite indicator originating in Europe. LIBOR is similar in effect to the Fed funds rate, but is a composite calculation of rates at which eighteen of the world's major banks actually *do* lend to each other, so isn't a target rate per se. While policy is used to try to influence LIBOR, it is much more a reflection of true lending and credit conditions, and has been adopted worldwide as an indicator. In the fall of 2008, at the height of the banking crisis, LIBOR spiked to stunning highs, showing the world just how bad credit conditions had become.

Why You Should Care

Target interest rates and the Fed funds rate will ultimately influence the interest rates, especially short-term rates, you will pay on loans or receive as income on deposits. Obviously, they will also affect the economy. Changes in the Fed funds rate are closely watched—as are the accompanying statements by the Fed—for signs of current economic stress and future economic direction.

32. FED OPEN MARKET OPERATIONS

The Fed funds rate is the Fed's most important tool for influencing economic activity and achieving price stability (see #31 Target Interest Rates). As it is a rate used by banks for lending to each other, the Fed does not control the rate directly, but does it instead through *open market operations*.

What You Should Know

With open market operations, the Fed adds or subtracts money from the economy, influencing the supply and demand balance for money and thus the interest rate, or price for that money. Open market operations are the method used by the Fed to bring the true Fed funds rate in line with the target rate, as well as to more directly moderate the amount of money in the system.

The operations consist of sale and purchase of mostly short-term U.S. government Treasury securities to and from the banks. If the Fed sells bonds, it drains money from the banks; if it buys bonds, that gives the banks money to lend. That additional money, multiplied through *leverage* (see #33 Fractional Reserve Banking), puts a lot more money into the financial system. The Fed does not mandate which securities to trade or which banks or dealers it will transact with; the market is "open" for banks and dealers to compete on price. Every day the Fed announces its intentions, and bond dealers and bankers mostly located in large Wall Street skyscrapers get to work dealing with the Federal Reserve Bank of New York's Domestic Trading Desk. The Federal Open Market Committee (FOMC), which also sets the target rates, monitors this activity.

Open market operations are usually very short term, dealing in short-term securities swapped back and forth on an almost overnight basis to fine-tune short-term interest rates. The Fed may also "jawbone" rates in one direction or another by making public statements in combination with actual open market operations. The persistent stimulus accomplished through the quantitative easing (QE3 and QE4) monthly purchase of $85 billion in bonds on the open market—and related publicity—serves as an excellent example.

Why You Should Care

Aside from the resulting influence on market interest rates, open market operations don't affect you directly. That said, if you were borrowing to buy a house or refinancing between 2011 and 2013, the well-communicated monthly bond-buying activities worked quite well to drive mortgage rates down to fifty-year lows. It's interesting to realize just how much goes on behind the scenes at the Fed and within the government in general to keep the economy moving in a favorable direction, and to smooth out the bumps. Without these operations we'd be looking at painful economic gyrations between inflation and deflation, or boom and bust, as seen in Figure 3.1.

33. FRACTIONAL RESERVE BANKING

Want to turn $100 into $500? Who wouldn't? And the architects and designers of the worldwide banking system have found just a way to do that—through so-called *fractional reserve banking*. Fractional reserve banking is a fundamental principle in modern-day banking whereby banks keep a fraction of their deposits in reserve and lend out the rest. Fractional reserve banking allows banks to stay in existence to make a profit on funds lent out. More importantly, in the aggregate, fractional reserve banking effectively creates more money for the economy.

What You Should Know

Unless governed by the terms of a certificate of deposit, the money people have deposited in a bank can be withdrawn at any time. So how can a bank lend out money to others and earn a profit if it might have to return money to its depositors at a moment's notice? Fractional reserve banking works on the theory that in all but the biggest crises, only a small fraction of depositors will want their money back.

This idea then turns banks loose to lend out the rest—directly to customers or to each other. When banks lend money to each other, the borrowing bank can keep a fraction of that loan and lend to still others—customers or banks—and the cycle repeats. By keeping only a fraction of the money in reserve, banks can lend the same money many times over, effectively increasing the supply of money through leverage. In aggregate, the supply of money is thus a multiple of the "base" money created by deposits—or by injections from a central bank. In practice, the amount of money in circulation can be five, ten, or even twenty times the amount injected into the banking system by the Fed or individual depositors.

This practice sounds risky, and indeed it can be, for if depositors see a crisis and demand all their money at once, it pulls the rug out from under the layers of leveraged loans. The Fed imposes a reserve requirement (see #36 Reserve Requirements) to mandate that banks keep at least a certain percentage of their deposits or funds in reserve to protect against bank runs.

But in the 2008 banking crisis, depositors became worried about their deposits in banks and withdrew in greater numbers, forcing a rapid contraction in reserves and in money to loan. The fear and contraction of lendable reserves fed on itself in a cycle of deleveraging (see #9 Deleveraging). Further, bank reserves were hit hard by bad investments, loan write-offs, and contracting asset values. The result was very restricted, or "tight," credit, and the banking system nearly ground to a standstill. The Fed and the U.S. Treasury had to step in to create money and bolster bank reserves through TARP, the Troubled Asset Relief Program. These problems were amplified by the leverage created through fractional reserve banking.

This is not to say that fractional reserve banking is a bad thing—it is really a good thing when managed properly. It puts more money in circulation, makes credit easier to obtain, and fosters economic growth. The problems occur when banks get careless in how they lend money; when that happens the multiplicative effect occurs in reverse.

Why You Should Care

Fractional reserve banking occurs largely in the background; under normal circumstances it won't affect your household finances or what you can pull from an ATM machine. But especially in the aftermath of the 2008–2009 banking crisis, it helps to understand what makes banks succeed or fail. Healthy banks lend money to you on favorable terms and keep the economy going. What happened during that period is a helpful reminder of the risks of using leverage to expand purchasing power.

34. REFLATION

Reflation is a term used somewhat informally in economics to refer to combined government efforts to stimulate an economy, particularly one hard hit by recession, deflation (see #19 Deflation), or an enduring decline in asset prices. The term is relevant in the aftermath of the Great Recession, as many economists felt that governments and the Fed in particular were engaging in deliberate actions to "reflate" the economy at the risk of creating runaway inflation later.

What You Should Know

When a government or central bank reflates an economy, it uses a combination of strong monetary stimulus (see #56 Monetary Policy and #17 Money Supply) and fiscal stimulus (see #55 Fiscal Policy) to radically encourage demand, and ultimately boost asset prices. In the aftermath of the crash of the real estate bubble, microscopic interest rates, trillions of dollars in direct capital infusions, bailouts, and tax rebates were all put into play to essentially inflate the prices of assets other than real estate.

Those price increases could ultimately make real estate relatively more attractive and affordable, especially if expanded economic activity also increased incomes. That, in theory, would stop the slide in real estate prices, halt the deleveraging, and bring back a stable banking system and economy. As we've seen, to a large degree these policies have worked.

The problem recognized by many economists is that once such policy is enacted, it is hard to "turn it off." The resulting inflation becomes a matter of expectation, and that makes it difficult to eliminate. (Note the fear and uncertainty in the markets in mid-2013 as the Fed announced "tapering" of its quantitative easing bond-buying activities.) Further, the excessive supply of money, or "liquidity," is hard to "mop up," especially if it becomes invested in longer-term real estate assets. Reflation may help save jobs and protect asset values for people vulnerable to a bust, but it may carry asset price distortions into the future, while making an economy more vulnerable to strong inflationary pressure later on. During the reflation period, for example, the prices of gold and bonds surged to new highs many thought to be excessive, and the prices of both have dropped to well off their peaks, although not everyone is calling it a "bubble" or a "crash"—at least so far.

Why You Should Care

Excessive inflation is an enemy to everyone except those who are in debt and can pay those debts later in cheaper dollars. Reflation policies can lead to excessive inflation; furthermore, they encourage more borrowing, which may put us back into the same position that caused Great Recession in the first place. When you see the government pull out all the stops to save an economy or to preserve the prices of overpriced assets, it's a sign of bad times now and greater economic risk in the future. Likewise, when you see the prices of certain assets like gold rise to new heights because of reflationary policies, look out, especially if the policy changes and you're still invested in these assets.

Many economists and investment professionals follow and recommend what they call the *reflation trade*. If rampant inflation is expected in a moderately growing economy, investors might want to avoid mainstream economies like the U.S. economy, where dollar depreciation and economic malaise will cripple the value of their investments. Since China is the world's premier growing economy at this point and must buy most of its resources overseas, it has been felt by many that Australian and Canadian currencies and companies might fare well in a reflation scenario. Their governments aren't forced to print money at this point, and they sell resources needed by the resource-hungry China and Asian world. Investments can be made in pure currencies or resource exporters, or simply local businesses like utilities paying dividends in local currency. Most recently, however, this investing "idea" has diminished in popularity, as China's growth for an assortment of reasons has slowed. It goes to show that overseas investing isn't for everyone, but this discussion shows the complicated, far-reaching, and international consequences of reflation, and how to prepare for it.

35. PARADOX OF THRIFT

The "paradox of thrift," more often referred to today as the "paradox of saving," was originally described by the famed economist John Maynard Keynes. It's a simple paradox: if more people save more money in a bad economy, that leads to a fall in aggregate demand, which makes the recession worse. This concept would have been easy to ignore—except that it became a big part of the story of the Great Recession.

What You Should Know

The paradox of thrift is something of a prisoner's dilemma—increased saving, which may be good for an individual, is bad for the economy as a whole. Clearly part of what caused the last bust was overspending and an overextension of credit, while personal savings rates dropped below zero (see #3 Saving and Investment). The natural reaction of people to the fear of losing assets or income, and a widespread new aversion to risk, was to stop spending and start saving. Savings rates jumped almost immediately to 5 percent before falling off to a more moderate 3 percent.

The paradox of thrift served to blunt the effects of economic stimulation and reflation (see #34 Reflation) because, as the Fed injected money into the economy, people just saved it for a "rainier" day. It didn't stimulate demand; thus it didn't stimulate production, and few were better off. The lesson: people spend and invest when they perceive opportunity worth the risk, not just when they have money available to spend. The lesson for policymakers is to fix what's causing the risk and let asset prices adjust; then the system is back in balance, and people won't hoard money out of fear.

A corollary thought: if policymakers want people to save, they should increase—not reduce—interest rates. That would motivate people to save; in today's environment the only thing that gets people to save is fear—that is not a path to economic health and well-being.

Why You Should Care

If you as an individual have cut your borrowing and spending, that's a good thing. When economists and policymakers complain about the paradox of thrift, that shouldn't influence you at all; it is not your responsibility to revive the economy!

36. RESERVE REQUIREMENTS

Reserve requirements oblige banks to keep a minimum fraction of their active demand deposits (largely, checking-account and other short-term account balances) set aside in reserve to meet customer withdrawals, written checks, and other routine transactions. The reserve requirement represents the "fraction" of the fractional reserve banking system (see #33) kept "at home" to meet customer demand.

What You Should Know

The Federal Reserve, specifically the Fed Board of Governors, mandates the reserve requirement. Today, it is 10 percent for transaction accounts exceeding $70.5 million at a given institution, and 3 percent for amounts between $12.4 million and $70.5 million. For the first $12.4 million, and for many other kinds of longer-term deposits like CDs or for corporate time deposits, the requirement is zero.

Such requirements make it easy for the banking system to generate considerable leverage, $10 or more for every $1 of deposits or Fed funds acquired. These requirements, however, are moderately high on an international scale; in the Eurozone the requirement is only 1 percent, and in the United Kingdom, Australia, and Canada, there is no set reserve requirement. This isn't to say that banks in other countries are less regulated; they are just regulated differently.

Why You Should Care

The low reserve requirements give banks a lot of power to lend and effectively create money, but it's easy to see how this leverage works the other way in times of crisis. Banks don't have much of a cushion to work with, and thus must rely on the Fed for bailouts.

37. LOAN LOSS RESERVE

Any smart business or individual should set aside an emergency reserve of some sort in case something unexpected happens. The previous entry covered reserve requirements—minimum capital set-asides required by the Federal Reserve to cover unexpected withdrawals. But are these reserves, ranging from 0 to 10 percent of assets, adequate? Reserve requirements are there to protect against unexpected withdrawals, but what about the bigger elephant in the room—the potential default on bank loans? Where is the capital cushion to cover these losses? Isn't this what really got us into the 2008–2009 credit crisis and the Great Recession that followed?

The short answer: indeed, banks were not sufficiently protected against bad loans. Banks do set aside so-called *loan loss reserves* to cushion against "normal" levels of loan defaults, but quite obviously most banks didn't set aside enough to cover what actually happened.

What You Should Know

Banks set aside loan loss reserves on the balance sheet as a "contra," or negative, asset. They book an expense every quarter known as a *loan loss provision* to put more funds in the reserve, then *charge off* the amount of a loan gone bad. The reserve helps avoid surprises. If a bank is accustomed to 1 percent of its loans going bad, and that amount indeed does go bad, the reserve covers it, and the charge-offs create no surprises in the financial statements. The bank remains healthy and continues to operate with the same amount of capital.

But if banks make riskier loans, or if their existing loans become more risky because of a declining economy, loan loss provisions should be increased by bank managers. They were, but probably not enough in these circumstances, as bank managers were reluctant to take even bigger hits to their bottom line by booking larger loan loss reserve provisions. As a result, bank capital positions declined, a factor leading to the bailouts that ultimately occurred.

Why You Should Care

Stronger, better-managed banks book adequate loan loss reserves to protect themselves, their depositors, and their shareholders. Growing loan loss reserves may reflect more conservative management—or may reflect a management worried about its loan portfolio. If you're thinking about doing business with a bank, and especially investing in a bank, be careful about banks with loan loss reserves less than industry averages (as a percent of a loan portfolio) or with growing reserves—unless they give a credible explanation. Finally, the idea of such a "rainy day fund" applies not only to banks, but to other businesses and your own personal finances, too.

38. TIER 1 CAPITAL

The U.S. banking system, like others around the world, depends on its ability to lend as much money as possible, several times the original owners' equity in the institution. If you have $1 to start a bank and can get $9 in customer deposits and/or loans from other banks or the Federal Reserve, you can lend out $10 to potential borrowers. You can make a lot of money on the $1 invested.

But what if one of your borrowers defaults on a $1 loan? You still owe your depositors $9, so your equity is wiped out. Perhaps you booked 1 percent as a loan loss reserve (see #37 Loan Loss Reserve), so you were prepared for a 10-cent loan to be written off. But $1? You're in bad shape. $1.50? You're out of business. This sort of scenario was common during the 2008–2009 banking crisis.

So if you're a bank regulator, what would you look for as a sign of bank safety? The 10-cent loan loss reserve? That's nice to have, and the larger the reserve the better. But is there a safety cushion beyond that? That's where Tier 1 capital comes into the picture.

What You Should Know

Tier 1 capital is essentially the net equity in a bank (assets minus liabilities) plus the loan loss reserves. While loan loss reserves are set up to handle *expected* losses, Tier 1 capital is a better metric of how safe a bank is against *unexpected* losses.

The Tier 1 capital level is used together with a risk-adjusted measure of a bank's loan portfolio to determine a *capital adequacy ratio (CAR)*, or the ratio of the capital level to the loan base adjusted for risk. Investment analysts and bank regulators monitor the CAR ratio for banks to evaluate safety and to compare banks. The Tier 1 capital and CAR ratio received publicity in the media in postcrisis coverage of big banks like Bank of America, JPMorgan Chase, Morgan Stanley, Goldman Sachs, Wells Fargo, and Citigroup. The Tier 1 capital level was also one of the ingredients in the "stress testing" conducted by the Federal Reserve.

Based on the Federal Deposit Insurance Act, the law governing deposit insurance (see #45 FDIC), banks must have a Tier

loan loss reserves vs. expected losses

Tier 1 - unexpected losses

1 CAR of at least 4 percent. Institutions with a ratio below 4 percent are considered undercapitalized, and those below 3 percent are significantly undercapitalized—but most investors and industry experts feel that a level closer to 10 percent is really adequate. Aligned to this thinking, in July 2013, the Federal Reserve Board recommended that the Tier 1 minimum for the eight "globally significant" U.S. banks be raised to 6 percent— and also announced that of the eight institutions in question, only Wells Fargo & Company currently complied with that measure.

Why You Should Care

Unless you're in the banking business or are a bank investor, you don't need to calculate Tier 1 ratios. But if you see a report that a major bank's Tier 1 ratio is declining, that bank may be in trouble—about to cut its dividend to shareholders, or about to raise capital by selling more shares in the markets (both bad for investors). As a depositor, there probably isn't much to worry about, because depositors only lose what is not covered by FDIC insurance, and after equity investors lose.

39. DODD-FRANK WALL STREET REFORM AND CONSUMER PROTECTION ACT OF 2010

It often takes crisis to bring change in American politics, and the Dodd-Frank Wall Street Reform and Consumer Protection Act of 2010 is a crystal-clear example. "Dodd-Frank," as it is more casually known, came to us as a direct consequence of the Great Recession. Introduced by Senate Banking Committee Chairman

Chris Dodd and House Financial Services Committee Chairman Barney Frank in 2009, the bill became law in 2010 and is aimed mainly at consolidating and strengthening regulation in the financial services industry.

What You Should Know

The new law brought sweeping changes to the investment, financial services, and consumer finance industries, many of which are too detailed and focused on industry internals to matter to most, unless you work in the industry. Much of the new law's provisions aim at avoiding or reducing the risks and regulating transactions central to the causes of the Great Recession. A new "Financial Stability Oversight Council" assesses risks and stresses, and provides for the Federal Reserve to more closely supervise "too big to fail" bank holding companies, giving us the "stress tests" occasionally reported in the news. An "Office of Financial Research" compiles data on the performance and risks of the financial system, and presents it to Congress, among others. New rules streamline the liquidation of banks, savings and loans, brokerages, and other financial institutions. The law beefs up reporting requirements for Registered Investment Advisers, and sets up new rules—and possibly a new regulatory body (still to be determined)—for hedge funds.

Importantly, the law as passed re-establishes the "Volcker Rule," separating commercial and investment banking operations, and restricting what banks can invest on their own accounts (so called "proprietary trading"). The law also called for new regulation and standardization of the trading of credit derivatives, especially credit default swaps (see #69 Credit Default Swap). New rules give greater authority to the Securities and Exchange Commission (see #44 SEC) on a number of fronts, including the establishment of a "whistleblower bounty program" to encourage discovery of unfair securities practices. New oversight is now given to the credit rating agencies— Standard & Poor's, Moody's, and Fitch—to prevent conflicts of interest and other practices that led to the misrating of credit securities before the crisis. Finally, Dodd-Frank established the Consumer Financial Protection Bureau, adding new and centralized regulation to financial products and services, including new disclosure requirements and educational materials, and putting former Harvard professor and outspoken consumer advocate, and now Massachusetts senator, Elizabeth Warren, in charge.

Why You Should Care

The far-reaching Dodd-Frank legislation should curb many of the excesses that caused the Great Recession, and also serves to centralize authority and regulation. That helps lawmakers (and you, if so interested) know whom to go to in order to understand the latest of what's happening in the industry, where the risks are, and to ensure compliance. For most of us, it's a security blanket to know that the government is watching, and that many critical areas in the financial industry are no longer reminiscent of the "Wild Wild West"—there's a new sheriff in town.

CHAPTER 5

Government and Government Programs

Whether or not you like the presence and cost of government, it plays a huge role in today's economy. Governments provide money and monitor its supply, but go way beyond to create and implement various policies and programs to influence the economy, fix the economy, spend critical resources, and make it better for all of us.

Government agencies regulate economic activity, providing safeguards and a fair and level playing field for economic transactions to occur. Certain bodies of law, like bankruptcy law, create fair ways to dissolve failed economic entities, ultimately facilitating the sort of risk-taking necessary to make the economy work in the first place.

Want to understand the role and importance of the government in the economy? Just try to picture what it would be like *without* government. We would have no universally accepted currency, and no supervision and regulation of the markets and other economic activity—and no reallocation of resources to

public programs and infrastructure, like roads and airports—
that make the greater economy work.

40. U.S. TREASURY

It's good to know where our money comes from and who's managing it. Today, it's sort of a joint venture between the Federal Reserve,
our central bank, and the U.S. Department of the Treasury.

The Treasury department is part of the executive branch of
the U.S. federal government and reports to the president. While
the Federal Reserve (see #30 Federal Reserve) was created in
1913, the Treasury has been with us almost since day one, being
created by Congress in 1789 to manage government revenue
and currency.

What You Should Know

The Federal Reserve and the U.S. Treasury work together to
create and implement money and monetary policy. The Federal
Reserve is more the "brains" of the operation, deciding what
policies to put into place with regard to employment, prosperity,
and price stability; the Treasury is more "working man," in place
to carry out the programs.

The Treasury prints, mints, and monitors all physical money
in circulation, including paper and coin currency. The U.S. Mint
and the Bureau of Engraving and Printing are part of the Treasury. In addition, the Treasury is responsible for all government
revenue generation through taxes—the Internal Revenue Service
is part of the Treasury. Beyond raising money through taxes, the
Treasury also raises money by creating debt securities—bills,

notes, and bonds—to sell to the general public, banks, corporations, investment funds, and so forth.

So if the Fed decides to increase money supply, the Treasury puts the plan into place, although the Fed can also create more money by injecting money into the banking system directly, and has done that a lot recently. If Congress decides to change tax policy, the Treasury (through the IRS) carries that policy out. The Treasury does not decide on tax policy, nor does it create or change tax law.

The Treasury also performs other roles, such as measuring economic activity; providing economic and budgetary advice for the executive branch, Fed, and others; and producing other revenue through alcohol and tobacco taxes, postage stamps, and so forth. Until 2003, the Treasury also handled firearms regulation, customs and duties, and the Secret Service, but these functions have been transferred to the departments of Justice and Homeland Security.

Why You Should Care

Aside from the fact that its building is on the back of the $10 bill, and its original secretary, Alexander Hamilton, is on the front, it's good to know what the Treasury is and does. Most of us have at least annual contact with the Treasury through the IRS at tax time. Additionally, it is the Treasury that issues U.S. securities, which we, or our banks or companies, may buy or sell occasionally. The Treasury carries out policies; it does not create them, so those that we agree or disagree with should be attributed to someone else in government. More recently, the Treasury and the Federal Reserve collaborated to create and implement federal bailout programs, like TARP, to safeguard the banking system from collapse and to strengthen it moving forward.

41. FEDERAL BUDGET

The federal budget, known more formally as the Budget of the United States Government, is a document prepared by the president and submitted to Congress for approval. The document outlines revenue, spending projections, and recommendations for the government fiscal year, which starts October 1 of the current year—so the 2013 federal budget covers the fiscal year beginning October 1, 2012 and ending September 30, 2013. Congress then adds its own budget resolutions (one each from the House and Senate). The budget is passed and signed into law; then individual appropriations bills are passed to actually fund government programs.

What You Should Know

The federal budget, by nature, outlines the nation's spending priorities and is used as a tool to manage and solve social and economic problems on a large and small scale. Budgets don't always cover emergencies, as discovered by additional fiscal year 2009 appropriations made for TARP and other economic relief in the wake of the financial crisis. Certain military operations like those in Iraq and Afghanistan may also be wholly or in part funded and administered outside the budget process.

The size of the federal budget has increased dramatically over the years. The 2013 budget calls for a budget of some $3.8 trillion, well more than double the 1999 level of $1.7 trillion. Some of that increase reflects inflation, but it also, more importantly, reflects an ever-growing role of government in the operation of our nation, as well as a continued solidifying and stimulating of the economic base in the wake of the financial crisis.

Has revenue growth kept up with spending growth? Indeed not; the 2013 deficit is projected at $901 billion, down from the $1.17 trillion in 2010 and the record $1.75 trillion in 2009. Budgets are typically construed as part of a longer-term plan, and President Obama had planned to reduce the deficit to $533 billion by 2013—but a lagging economic recovery and failure to resolve "gridlock" over tax and spending policy have delayed that reduction. The deficit that remains is still substantially larger than those of the worst years of the Bush administration. That said, the Bush budgets do not account for expenditures that occurred largely outside the budget—for example, the wars in Iraq and Afghanistan, which were funded by supplemental appropriations bills, instead of the original budget or routine appropriations process.

It's interesting to look at the specific areas of revenue and expense in the 2013 budget, and how those specifics compare to the recession-riddled year 2010. Note the effects of the rebounded economy and the $80 billion in interest "income" derived from bonds purchased in Fed open market operations:

REVENUES ($2.902 TRILLION, (+21.9% VS. 2010))

- $1.359 trillion: Individual income taxes (+28.1%)
- $959 billion: Social Security, other payroll taxes (+2.0%)
- $348 billion: Corporate income taxes (+56.8%)
- $88 billion: Excise taxes (+14.3%)
- $33 billion: Customs duties (+43.5%)
- $13 billion: Estate and gift taxes (-35.0%)
- $80 billion: Deposits of earnings and Federal Reserve System (not previously separated out)
- $21 billion: Other (-44.7%)

Unfortunately, so-called "mandatory" expenditures continue to grow, and will probably do so until "entitlement reform" actually takes place. Sizeable increases in the Social Security, Medicare/Medicaid, and Interest on the National Debt lines drive the mandatory spending increase:

MANDATORY SPENDING (MANDATORY SPENDING: $2.293 TRILLION (+5.0% VS. 2010))

- $820 billion (+18.0%): Social Security
- $860.3 billion (+15.8%): Medicare and Medicaid
- $246 billion (+50.0%): Interest on National Debt

Some restraint on spending growth is evident in the "discretionary" side:

DISCRETIONARY SPENDING ($1.510 TRILLION (+10.4% VS. 2010))

- $666.2 billion (+0.4%): Department of Defense (including Overseas Contingency Operations)
- $80.6 billion (+2.4%): Department of Health and Human Services
- $67.7 billion (+45.0%): Department of Education
- $60.4 billion (+15.0%): Department of Veterans Affairs
- $56.1 billion (+8.5%): Department of State and Other International Programs
- $54.9 billion (+28.6%): Department of Homeland Security
- $41.1 billion (–13.8%): Department of Housing and Urban Development

Note that these are just the seven largest line items: there are twenty-one more line items, some as large as cabinet departments, some more specific, such as $7.4 billion for the National Science Foundation.

Why You Should Care

Just as you should care about your own income and spending and budget accordingly to make ends meet, you also should care about whether the government is doing the same thing—whether it is using your tax dollars appropriately, and making good decisions. Budget talk can be contentious at certain times, dull at others, and complex always, but it's in your best long-term interest to keep tabs on what's happening. Budgets are usually proposed early in a calendar year; you should find a favorite news source and keep track of them. Budget detail is available at the U.S. Government Printing Office "GPO Access" website from the Office of Management and Budget—see *www.gpo.gov/fdsys/browse/collectionGPO.action?collectionCode=BUDGET*. The current and upcoming year's budget documents, while long, are always an interesting read.

42. FEDERAL DEFICITS AND DEBT

After reading the previous entry on the U.S. federal budget, you might understandably be concerned about the excess of expenditures over revenue, and what that might mean for you and for the economy. Put simply, if *you* spent that much more than you earned, you'd be in big trouble—deep in debt or worse.

What You Should Know

Truth is, the size of the federal deficit and the load of debt it has created is of great concern, especially to fiscally conservative politicians and citizens. Such large deficits and debts sap our future economic strength and may hinder our ability to borrow, as we must service—that is, pay—interest and principal on our current debt. There was great concern that because of already existing debts, the United States may not be able to borrow its way out of the recent economic crisis and downturn. So far, those problems haven't materialized, as U.S. debt obligations are still considered among the world's most secure. China in particular needs to support our economy because of the degree to which our economy supports its economy. Now the concern is about what happens next time around, when we're still further in debt.

Figure 5.1 speaks for itself. You can see the tremendous bulge in the size of the deficit and the increase in the national debt that occurred in 2009, as federal programs were put into play to alleviate the effects of the Great Recession. Economists consider part of the deficit as *structural*, recurring as part of government's overall initiatives and priorities, and some of it as *cyclical*, as in the medicine applied to fix the banks, reduce unemployment, and so forth. You can see that as some of the economic stimulus takes hold, the deficits and increases in debt are declining slowly, but still considerably exceed earlier figures, and for that matter, any time in history.

Figure 5.1 Projected Deficits and Debt Increases, 2001–2012

Total Deficits vs. National Debt Increases

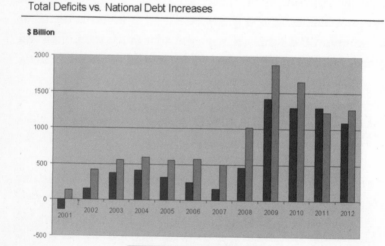

Source: Congressional Budget Office, U.S. Treasury

If there is any good news about deficits and debt, it is that they are still moderate compared to the size of the national economy. Government spending in the United States runs about 25 percent of GDP, compared to figures of 50 percent and higher for many other developed Western nations. The deficits, while huge in absolute dollars, have run somewhere in the range of 3 to 5 percent of GDP historically—again, not a large number on the world stage, but with the recent increases in the deficits and accompanying moderation in GDP growth, the figure has risen to 6.2 percent most recently.

Why You Should Care

Different people feel differently about being in debt. Clearly, the rising levels of debt "put the burden on our children," but that's been said for years. It's alarming to think that our national debt runs about $52,953 per person (that's $212,000 for a family of four, up about 60 percent since 2009)—if you ran up such debt on your own you'd be in big trouble! But the government can print money, and other nations find it in their interest to support our debt. Inflation may take some of the sting out of the debt as well (see #34 Reflation). But it is still a big elephant in the room, one to be concerned about for the future, and it argues for all of us to reduce our spending habits and not get carried away trying to prevent economic downturns (see #59 Austrian School).

43. SECURITIES ACTS OF 1933, 1934, AND 1940

While the Great Recession was a big deal, and new legislation has emerged from it (see #39 Dodd-Frank), so far it has not been a watershed for new securities and investment laws, as were the 1929 stock market crash and the Great Depression. Those events brought Congress to pass a series of laws to regulate the heretofore largely unregulated securities industry. Many newer laws have come onto the scene, but the four "biggies" remain the set passed in 1933, 1934, and 1940.

What You Should Know

The four laws listed below set the ground rules for selling securities to the public and for trading those securities, and for investment companies and professional investment advisers. They also set up and defined the role for the Securities and Exchange Commission (see #44 SEC).

- *Securities Act of 1933* was designed to limit outright securities fraud; it requires disclosure of financial information for securities brought to public sale. It also prohibits "deceit, misrepresentation, or fraud" in the sale of securities. It is sometimes called the "truth in securities" law.

- *Securities Exchange Act of 1934* did two things. First, it created the SEC and empowered it to register, regulate, and oversee brokerage firms and firms otherwise dealing in securities transactions, and also set up a system whereby it could extend its reach by aligning with industry trade organizations like the Financial Industry Regulatory Authority (FINRA), formerly the National Association of Securities Dealers (see #82 Brokers, Broker Dealers, and RIAs), and the securities exchanges themselves. Second, it required regular financial reporting to holders of corporate securities.

- *Investment Company Act of 1940* regulates so-called investment companies—companies set up to invest in securities and then sell their own shares to the investing public. This law set the ground rules for mutual funds. Those ground rules include tax-free pass-through of income, a requirement that at least 90 percent of income generated is paid out, and limits to sales charges and fees. If you own a mutual fund, that fund is designed within and regulated by this law.

- *Investment Advisers Act of 1940* regulates professional investment advisers. This law requires advisers, within certain definitions and limits, to register with the SEC and conform to regulations designed to protect investors.

These laws provide a framework, but aren't absolute in nature; the SEC can and does have authority to add rules to these laws to close gaps and accommodate new technology and methods.

Why You Should Care

While it's easy to think that financial firms, investment funds, and advisers got away with murder during the recent crisis, you should know that there is a fairly substantial framework in which they operate. That said, the shortcomings of the SEC became apparent. As a prudent individual, you should always make sure any investment adviser you deal with is registered.

These laws don't cover everything in the investment markets. If you're thinking about hedge funds (see #72), realize they largely escape this framework because they are targeted toward certain qualified individuals, not the public at large. As we found out with the recent failure of MF Global, a commodities trading firm run by former New Jersey governor Jon Corzine, they don't apply to commodities trading, either. That may change, and new laws may also emerge to counteract scandals like the Bernard Madoff debacle.

44. SECURITIES AND EXCHANGE COMMISSION (SEC)

The Securities and Exchange Commission is an independent public agency within the U.S. government, chartered primarily to enforce the major securities laws outlined in the previous entry. The SEC is a vital referee in a game that, without referees, might well go out of control, although it has been on the hot seat for some important "no-calls" and bad officiating in recent years.

What You Should Know

The SEC is a large and complex organization, but much of it is organized in the following four major groups, three of which loosely align with the major securities laws covered above:

- *Division of Corporation Finance* primarily oversees proper disclosure of regular financial information to the public, like annual and quarterly reports and other required filings, and so centers its activities on the 1933 law.
- *Division of Trading and Markets* concerns itself with "maintaining fair, orderly, and efficient" markets. As such, this division makes sure exchanges, brokers, and others involved in trading securities follow the rules, especially those set forth in the 1934 law.
- *Division of Investment Management* ensures proper registration and disclosure for funds, investment advisers, and investment managers—primarily the 1940 laws.
- *Division of Enforcement* investigates violations and takes civil or administrative action when appropriate.

The SEC got into trouble in the aftermath of the Bernard Madoff scandal. In its defense, it simply doesn't have the staff to properly police the rapidly expanding and ever-faster-moving securities markets. The staff of 4,000 must sift through 90,000 complaints brought to the SEC each year; out of these, some 794 enforcement actions took place in 2012. In addition to the complaints coming in, staff has a responsibility to examine things on its own to ensure compliance. Some still say the SEC is too cozy with big players, choosing to assume they're right or to look the other way, while spending too much time enforcing registration and other minor compliance issues with smaller brokers and dealers. Under the leadership of Chair Mary Jo White, and with the backing of certain provisions of the Dodd-Frank Wall Street Reform and Consumer Protection Act of 2010 (See #39), the agency has taken many steps, including hiring more agents and reviewing internal processes, to deal with these issues. Today's SEC is generally considered more aggressive in its investigation and enforcement of compliance within the securities industry

Why You Should Care

The SEC, while under fire from Congress and the general public, plays a vital role in ensuring the safety and integrity of your investments. It's helpful to know what the SEC does, and how your key investments and "nest egg" are protected. It is also important to know that the SEC *won't*—and *shouldn't*— prevent you from losing money in the securities markets, so long as everything that happens is within the law.

45. FEDERAL DEPOSIT INSURANCE CORPORATION (FDIC)

The banking collapse in the Great Depression, during which some 20 percent of all banks failed and their customer deposits were gone forever, led to new protections of deposits. As part of the Glass-Steagall Act of 1933, the Federal Deposit Insurance Corporation was set up within the government to guarantee deposits meeting certain criteria. As a bank depositor, your deposits are most likely covered, and would be paid back in the event of a bank failure, but it's worth reviewing the rules.

What You Should Know

Today, deposits are covered up to $250,000 *per depositor per bank* for most types of checking and savings accounts. This amount was raised from $100,000 during the 2008 banking crisis. The "per depositor per bank" rule makes it fairly easy to achieve greater levels of coverage; you can have one account and your spouse can have another at the same bank, and both are covered. Or you can have joint accounts at two separate banks (they must be completely separate—not Wells Fargo and subsidiary Wachovia, for example). If you have several accounts at one bank, the coverage considers the *total*, not each account separately.

If you have millions, there are ways to extend this coverage further by having an intermediary spread your accounts through the Certificate of Deposit Account Registry Service (CDARS). If you have millions in savings, check out *www.cdars.com*. If you're more like the rest of us, with a few accounts, the FDIC ownership and coverage rules can be found at the FDIC's website: *www .fdic.gov/deposit/deposits/insured/ownership.html*.

One thing to remember: FDIC does *not* cover investment accounts. The most common example used for savings is money market *funds* (not to be confused with so-called money market *accounts*, a product offered by some banks that *is* covered.). Some funds, however, might be covered by *optional* insurance offered by the U.S. Treasury in the wake of the 2008 banking crisis. The FDIC doesn't cover credit union accounts per se, but the National Credit Union Share Insurance Fund (NCUSIF) offers nearly identical coverage.

Investment accounts are covered by SIPC (Securities Investor Protection Corporation) for up to $500,000, but this coverage is against failure of the broker, not investment losses, and so rarely applies.

Why You Should Care

It is very important, especially in this day and age of financial volatility, to have at least some security for your savings. You should ask questions and take the necessary steps to ensure that your core savings are covered. It's worth keeping track of changes in the laws too.

46. GOVERNMENT-SPONSORED ENTERPRISES (GSES)

Government-sponsored enterprises have been created by Congress over the years, starting during the Depression-era New Deal, to provide credit to targeted sectors of the economy like farming, housing, and education. The most visible GSEs today are Fannie Mae (once called the Federal National Mortgage Association, now officially called Fannie Mae) and Freddie Mac, once the Federal Home Loan Mortgage Corporation. Other GSEs include the Farm Credit System created in 1916, and Sallie Mae, once the Student Loan Marketing Association, created in 1972. Sallie Mae is no longer a GSE; it became the private SLM Corporation during the period 1997–2004.

What You Should Know

For almost all of us, the two mortgage finance GSEs and the twelve additional Federal Home Loan Banks are most important. These institutions have created what's known as the secondary mortgage market, buying mortgages from mortgage bankers and other lenders, and repackaging and selling them as mortgage-backed securities into the financial markets. This activity provides greatly expanded liquidity in the mortgage markets and thus makes mortgages much more "available" and affordable for all of us. These institutions also "guarantee" certain loans, making them more attractive to investors, and thus lowering the interest rates and qualification requirements.

Before the 2008 financial crisis, the GSEs were pressured by policymakers to make more loans more affordable for more people to accomplish stated federal government goals to expand U.S. home ownership. This led to deterioration in credit quality requirements (that is, the standards applied to borrowers for income, credit ratings, and general ability to pay). This relaxation in standards expanded the market for so-called subprime mortgages; the GSEs and many institutions they sold to took a big hit when these mortgages started to fail. The GSEs, most of which had existed since the late 1960s as standalone publicly traded stock companies, had to be largely taken over and "bailed out" by the federal government, an act consistent with their original GSE charters, but something of a shock to the financial markets.

GSEs, specifically Fannie Mae and Freddie Mac, are not explicitly guaranteed by the federal government. This issue was tested in late 2008 as these two GSEs were caught with bad loan portfolios, and the question arose as to whether they would "make good" on guarantees and loans they had given or sold to others. The government didn't do that, but essentially took them over by putting them into a conservatorship, wiping out private investor equity, and they still do function today, but at a diminished level. Their future is still being debated.

Why You Should Care

Fannie Mae and Freddie Mac still ultimately buy, repackage, and sell a healthy portion of home mortgages granted in the United States today.

Additionally, Fannie Mae and Freddie Mac set the limit on the maximum size of a loan they consider "conventional"—that is, eligible for preferred interest rates and guarantees. Until 2008, that limit was $417,000; a mortgage exceeding that amount was said to be "not conforming," and thus would be a "jumbo" loan having higher interest rates—currently 1 to 1.5 percent higher. In 2008, the GSEs raised the limit to $625,500, depending on geography.

47. TAX POLICY AND INCOME TAXATION

The proper coverage of the subject of taxation obviously would take more than a single entry. The Government Printing Office reported in 2006 that the U.S. Income Tax Code, the body of law administered by the Internal Revenue Service, was 13,548 pages in length. Additional rulings, opinions, and supplemental documents run the total up to about 44,000. And that's just U.S. income taxes—there are other kinds of taxes like sales (consumption), excise, estate, and many others. It's a complex subject.

What You Should Know

Taxation is obviously designed to raise revenue for governments and public entities to fund their operations and for redistribution—that is, to move money to needy parts of society in the form of entitlements like Social Security and Medicare and other direct and indirect aid programs (see #50 Entitlements). Considerable debate has occurred over how much of this is appropriate.

Income taxation began in 1861 in the United States to pay for the Civil War—the rate was a flat 3 percent on incomes exceeding $800. It went away after the war but returned briefly in 1894, and more permanently in 1913 as the Sixteenth Amendment. It's been with us, with much change and increased complexity, ever since. Regarding income taxation and tax policy, a few fundamental principles are important:

- Income taxation is *progressive*. Following the edict "from each according to his ability," rates go up the higher your taxable income. Just how progressive is a subject of tax policy; as of this writing the current top tax rate is 39.6 percent, but has been as high as 92 percent (1952–53). Of course, how much tax you pay is defined not just by the rate but by how much of your income is taxable.

- Tax policy is *fiscal policy*. The federal government can—and has—used tax policy to stimulate the economy, as was most famously done in the Reagan years with a dramatic lowering of top, or marginal, rates and average tax rates paid. The top income tax rate was lowered from 70 percent to 50 percent in 1982 and again to 33 percent in 1987. It has varied between 33 percent and 39.6 percent ever since. It is felt that a lower top rate does two things: first, it gets wealthier and higher-income people to invest in the economy, thus providing jobs and creating more tax revenue downstream; second, it reduces the amount of effort made to avoid taxes!

- The IRS does not create tax law. Congress creates tax law; the IRS merely *enforces* it. Also, doing the most you can within the law to *avoid* taxes is considered a good thing; it is neither the intent of Congress nor the IRS that you pay taxes that you don't owe. Evasion is when you knowingly try to get around taxes that you *do* owe, and that's where severe consequences can result.

Why You Should Care

Current tax policy and laws naturally determine how much of your income—all forms of it—you're entitled to keep. Most view taxes as a necessary evil, and are resigned to pay whatever their accountants say they owe. With a deeper understanding of taxes and how they might affect your current financial situation, you can take charge and *plan* your taxes so as to minimize them. That is also a good thing, and encouraged by the IRS. Just as you would budget a business or your personal finances, it pays to put some energy into saving money on taxes—taxes of all types, from all jurisdictions. Don't be afraid to do this.

48. CREDIT PROTECTION

The dangers of unfair credit practices, or "lawlessness" in this area, are obvious—it's too easy for unknowing or unsuspecting people to be "sold" on the idea of borrowing money to buy something under unreasonable terms. The federal government has passed an assortment of laws over time to make credit practices more consistent, fair, and understandable. In making things fair, they help the economy function more efficiently, as people can trust lenders to a greater degree—and vice versa.

What You Should Know

Federal laws serve mainly to clarify the responsibilities of creditors and debtors in consumer credit relationships, although the most recent 2009 legislation goes a bit farther by providing ground rules for what credit card companies can and can't do. Here are four of the most important laws governing credit and credit fairness:

1. **TILA—***Truth in Lending Act.* This act hit the books in 1968, and since that time has had a handful of revisions. TILA is mostly about disclosure, and for all types of consumer lending, requires written disclosure upfront of lending terms, cost of credit (annualized percentage rate, or APR), fees, and so forth. TILA has been amended more recently to require specific disclosures for adjustable-rate mortgages and reverse mortgages. TILA also allows a three-day "rescission" period to cancel any loan, and a three-year "extended right to rescind" if disclosures aren't made properly.

2. **FCBA—***Fair Credit Billing Act.* This 1986 law covers the fair disclosure and billing of credit card accounts, and covers such topics as how to dispute a charge and cardholder liability in the event of unauthorized use (setting a maximum liability of $50).

3. **FCRA—***Fair Credit Reporting Act.* The FCRA of 1970 covers your rights to review, fix, or authorize others to use your credit report and score. Key features include the process to dispute and resolve reporting, the requirement to

give you a free credit report once a year, and a score (not necessarily free) when you want it. You also have some control over who can use the score, including the ability to opt out of using your credit rating as a factor in insurance and credit company solicitations.

4. **FDCPA—*Fair Debt Collection Practices Act.*** Finally, this 1977 law covers what collectors can and can't do, including hours and means of contact, and disclosure of your debt problems. It's not hard to find out more about these laws by simple online search. The Federal Trade Commission consumer protection site also helps; see: *www.consumer.ftc.gov/topics/credit-and-loans.*

A few years ago, Congress passed the Credit Card Accountability, Responsibility, and Disclosure (CARD) Act of 2009. This is a broad credit cardholder's "bill of rights" limiting the ability of credit card companies to raise interest rates without adequate notice or triggers, and dealing with a host of other consumer-unfriendly practices in the credit card industry. As a user of credit and especially if you have a lot of credit cards, you should understand this new law.

Why You Should Care

While most credit problems are corrected by getting spending habits under control and making required payments, mistakes or aggressive creditor practices do happen, and sometimes it makes sense to consider your legal options. Like any game, it helps to know the rules and how to cry "foul." You should learn what questions to ask and how to communicate with creditors, but don't expect the law to mitigate the effects of bad habits.

49. BANKRUPTCY LAW

Everybody makes mistakes. In the old days, if you ran out of money or your debts exceeded your assets, you would be sent to debtors' prison—or worse. What would happen if debtors' prison existed today? Very simply, people wouldn't take risks, and they wouldn't spend money. If people didn't take risks, we wouldn't have the conveniences and technologies we have today. And people wouldn't spend money at all for fear of that cold, dark debtors' prison.

The bankruptcy process and set of laws around it are designed to clean up people's financial mistakes in a fair and equitable way. While bankruptcy certainly isn't good for the individual or company going through it, it stops short of being a draconian, desperate measure. So yes, bankruptcy is a bad thing, especially for the individuals and companies involved. But the way the process is set up actually helps the economy.

What You Should Know

Bankruptcy happens when an individual or corporation declares its inability to pay its creditors (voluntary bankruptcy), or when a creditor files a petition on behalf of a debtor to start the process (involuntary bankruptcy). The U.S. Constitution puts bankruptcy under federal jurisdiction, and a uniform Bankruptcy Code sets the rules, with some state amendments. Bankruptcy proceedings occur in federal court.

The most often used and discussed chapters in the Bankruptcy Code are Chapters 7, 11, and 13:

- Chapter 7: used by both individuals and corporations; leads to a simple and total liquidation of assets to pay creditors.

- Chapter 11: mostly occurs in the corporate sector, and leads to a reorganization and recapitalization of the company, usually with creditors receiving some portion of their debts in a predetermined order of priority.
- Chapter 13: for individuals; does not liquidate all assets but rather creates a payment plan to discharge the bankruptcy individually.

Bankruptcy usually allows certain property, such as personal effects and clothing, to be exempt from liquidation; these rules can vary by state. Chapter 7 rules allow only one bankruptcy filing in eight years, and during that eight-year period your credit rating and your ability to borrow will be severely impaired. Specific rules cover spousal property. In Chapter 13, the debtor doesn't forfeit assets, but must give up a portion of future income over the next three to five years. In Chapter 11, the business continues to run while creditors and debtors work out a deal in bankruptcy court. Eventually a plan is presented to the debtors, who must approve it.

Legislation in 2005, known as the Bankruptcy Abuse Prevention and Consumer Protection Act, made it harder for debtors with means to simply file and walk away; they must discharge their debts if they can. There was a large "bubble" of bankruptcy filings before this law went into effect. Even with this law, bankruptcy filings have been on the rise over the years, as consumer debt and the likelihood of catastrophic medical bills has increased. Many Chapter 13 filings allow a complete discharge of medical debt alongside the payment plan for ordinary debts. The economic crisis, not surprisingly, triggered a rise in business and personal bankruptcies. According to federal statistics, nonbusiness bankruptcy cases rose from about a million in 2008 to over 1.5 million in 2010; they are projected to drop to a level near 1 million for 2013.

Why You Should Care

Even with the protection that bankruptcy affords, you don't want to go there if you don't have to. That said, it's good to know that there's a fair and reasonably unthreatening way to settle insolvency should it ever become your unfortunate circumstance. So if you're planning to build and market that breakthrough electric car, go for it—you won't go to jail if you fail. And while prudence in personal finance and consumer debt is always the best path, if you lose a job or have a major medical catastrophe, bankruptcy does give you a way to deal with it.

50. ENTITLEMENTS: SOCIAL SECURITY AND MEDICARE

Entitlements, or "social insurance" programs, are designed to stabilize the economy in several ways. First, they allow people to retire with some degree of financial security, else they would have to keep working well into advancing age. That would, of course, not be good for them or their employers, and it would fill jobs that would otherwise be available for younger employees. Second, these programs take the burden of caring for elder family members off younger family members.

What You Should Know

Social Security is a child of the Great Depression, an era where some 50 percent of citizens over sixty-five reportedly lived below the poverty line. The program stands largely as originally conceived and passed in 1935. The most important component is the Old-Age, Survivors and Disability Insurance program, or OASDI. Benefits are paid for retirement, disability, survivorship, and death. Retirement and survivorship are the most substantial parts of the program; disability benefits are difficult to qualify for, and the death benefit is minimal.

When a citizen reaches a certain age, a retirement benefit is calculated based on work and earnings history. The "full retirement" age was once sixty-five, but now has been extended depending on birth date. A reduced benefit can be taken starting at age sixty-two; if the retiree chooses to defer benefits to age seventy, those benefits increase. Both adjustments are done by spreading a projected benefit over a different number of years; that is, the total projected benefit is the same, just divided differently. In rough numbers, the payout increases 8 percent for each year you delay retirement. The Social Security Administration has an informative website covering benefits and other topics; see *www.ssa.gov*.

Social Security is funded by the so-called FICA tax (which stands for Federal Insurance Contributions Act) taken from every paycheck or collected as "self-employment tax" from self-employed individuals. The FICA tax, which combines Social Security and Medicare, is 15.3 percent of gross income; in the case of employees, employers pay half. Of that amount, 12.4 percent is for Social Security; the remaining 2.9 percent is for Medicare. Social Security funds are collected on the first $113,700 of gross income, while Medicare collections have no limits. In addition, Congress passed an additional Medicare tax of 0.9 percent for individual earnings over $200,000, which now also includes "unearned" income (from investments, etc.).

The Social Security funds collected go into the Social Security trust funds. Those funds are used to pay current beneficiaries and to buy U.S. Treasury debt obligations—that is, to fund current deficits. Currently receipts exceed payouts, but many economists are concerned that the trust funds are a giant Ponzi scheme—that future receipts will go to support current recipients, leaving insufficient money for future retirees who are currently paying in. Social Security is the world's largest government program, and continues to represent about 20 percent of overall U.S. government expenditures.

Medicare, the "single-payer" health insurance and care program for those over sixty-five, came into existence in 1965. Medicare benefits are divided into four groups. Summarizing the four parts:

- Part A provides basic hospitalization, and is free for seniors otherwise eligible for Social Security—those who have paid into the trust funds for forty quarters (ten years).
- Part B provides outpatient benefits such as doctor's office visits and other care, and costs $104.90 per month in 2013 for individuals earning $85,000 or less, $170,000 filing jointly (rising to $325.70 monthly for individuals with over $214,000 in income, $428,000 filing jointly), a premium typically deducted from the Social Security Benefit.
- Part C, or "Medicare Advantage," was created in 1997 to help those who had private coverage through an employer health benefit plan or who chose to purchase such coverage; the benefits are modified to dovetail with such a plan, and often include items otherwise not included, like prescription drug coverage.
- Part D is a prescription drug benefit started in 2006 and costs $31.17 per month, again rising for higher earners.

Beyond Medicare, Medicaid provides additional benefits and pays some of the deductibles for seniors in serious financial need. Unlike Medicare, Medicaid programs can also cover qualifying needy families, and are administered at the state level; each state has different rules, although most of the funding is from the federal government. Typically, eligible seniors must have no more than a few thousand dollars in assets in addition to a home or car to qualify.

Why You Should Care

Beyond plugging what could be a huge—and growing—gap in the economy, these entitlement programs are important for your future financial planning. It's a good idea to develop a basic understanding of Social Security benefits (the annual statements they send you are helpful) and of Medicare before you reach your golden years.

51. RETIREMENT PLANS

Someday you're going to retire. And when that day comes, you should be eligible for Social Security, assuming you're at least sixty-two when you decide to leave that cubicle or workshop for good. But most financial experts expect that Social Security will only cover 20 to 50 percent of your income needs, especially if you are still paying for or renting a home.

That's where retirement savings plans come in.

What You Should Know

First, it's important to distinguish retirement *plans* from retirement *planning*. Retirement *plans* are special savings plans set up in the eyes of the law to provide tax incentives both for you and your employer to induce greater savings. They are also set up to be legally at "arm's length" from your employer, so that your savings cannot be tapped or otherwise manipulated should your employer get into trouble. That's important in these days of economic crisis and rapidly changing corporate (and public sector) fortunes.

Retirement *planning* is the active pursuit and calculation of your retirement needs, and how those needs will be funded in retirement—which you can do yourself if you have the skills, or with the help of a professional adviser.

There are three types of retirement savings plans. The first two are offered and administered through employers:

Defined benefit plans, as the name implies, specify the benefit. For example, you and your surviving spouse will receive $2,000 a month for as long as you live, come heck or high water. Your employer funds the plan, and its investments usually are managed by a third party; how they come up with enough to pay you is their problem. Traditional pension plans, as offered by most government agencies and legacy corporations, are defined benefit plans. These plans are going out of style because companies don't want the burden of extra funding for the plans in bad times. The Pension Benefit Guaranty Corporation, a government corporation set up to guarantee pension benefits, estimates there were 22,697 such plans in effect in early 2013, down from 80,000 such plans in the United States in 2005, and down from 250,000 in 1980. If you have a defined benefit plan, consider yourself fortunate.

Defined contribution plans, on the other hand, define the employee (and employer) contribution—what goes in—not the benefit that comes out. The widely used 401(k) plan is most common, allowing an employee to set aside up to $17,500 in funds each year, with an additional catch-up amount of $5,500 for employees over 50 years of age; some company plans offer matching funds. Public entities use 403(b) plans as an equivalent, and there are many other flavors. You must understand that the benefits you realize from these plans are both a function of how much you set aside *and* how well your investments perform; there are no guarantees. This lack of guarantee is of considerable concern to economists and savvy individuals alike; there is no assurance that retirees in the future will have sufficient funds to retire on, regardless of how much they set aside. Hit by the triple whammy of reduced earnings, lower stock prices, and increased emergency withdrawals, the Great Recession created a large drop in 401(k) balances to an average of $30,200 across 17,000 corporate 401(k) plans, according to plan administrator Fidelity Investments. More positively, that number recovered to an average of $75,900 by 2012, with sizable increases in employer and employee contributions along the way.

The third type, as the name implies, are individually set up and administered—*individual retirement plans, or "arrangements" (IRAs)*. These plans behave like defined contribution plans, except there is no connection to an employer. You set them up and fund them yourself. They have different tax advantages—traditional IRAs allow you to deduct contributions if you qualify, and pay taxes upon withdrawal; Roth IRAs don't allow the deduction, but withdrawals (including investment gains) are tax-free. Many people use these individual arrangements to supplement employer-sponsored plans, subject to specific rules. As with other defined contribution plans, there are no guarantees, except in the case of the failure of the broker or institution with which you have the account. With some exceptions, individuals can contribute $5,500 per year, $6,500 if over fifty. These accounts are widely used but not that deeply funded—in the wake of the financial crisis it was estimated that 75 percent of individuals nearing retirement age had less than $30,000 in their retirement accounts.

Why You Should Care

It pays to know what kind of retirement savings plans you have or are available to you, and to make the best use of them. While there is no single source or website that covers the entire gamut of resources, some consumer-friendly brokerages, like Fidelity (*www.fidelity.com*), get pretty close. Providing for retirement involves two steps: *retirement planning* to arrive at your needs, and *retirement savings plans* to get you there. For most, this two-step process is best done with a professional who has the tools and knowledge of the laws and plans, as well as your finances, to help you make the right decisions.

52. UNEMPLOYMENT BENEFITS

When unemployment rates double to over 10 percent in one year as they did during the Great Recession, obviously there's a big impact on the economy. Not only does the absence of income hurt the one in ten who aren't working, but it also hurts the economy at large, which of course leads to more unemployment. Thus, unemployment insurance, or "Jobseeker's Allowance," as it's called in the United Kingdom, helps to stabilize the economy and reduce the effects of boom and bust cycles.

As part of the 1935 Social Security Act in the wake of the Great Depression, unemployment insurance and benefits were established to help people through such times of general strife—or individual strife inherent in the transition of an individual company or industry. Although no longer part of Social Security, these benefits continue today and have been bolstered to a degree to mitigate the effects of the Great Recession.

What You Should Know

Today's unemployment insurance programs are actually a joint venture of the federal government and the states. They are funded through employer-paid payroll taxes paid to the states and to the federal government; the federal funds are then reallocated back to the states. The federal unemployment tax is collected under the Federal Unemployment Tax Act (FUTA) from most employers, exceptions being made for small companies with few employees. The base FUTA tax is 6.0 percent of the first $7,000 in wages. You won't see this tax on your paycheck; it is paid by the employer. State taxes vary by state, and may offset some federal taxes. FUTA funds are then given back to the states to administer unemployment and jobs programs, and to fund state-paid benefits.

Benefits are paid as a percentage of wages up to a maximum, and are typically available for twenty-six weeks upon filing a valid claim. Legislation may be invoked during bad times to extend benefits, as was the case in late 2008, and benefit periods have been extended since. Eligibility varies by state. To find the rules in your state, one resource is the "CareerOneStop" locator, maintained in conjunction with the U.S. Department of Labor, at *www.servicelocator.org/OWSLinks.asp*.

Why You Should Care

Most people get through their working lives without having to file for unemployment benefits, but obviously they can help a great deal in times of stress. Particularly if you feel your job is in jeopardy, it's worth knowing about the rules *before* something bad happens—that way, you can plan, for instance, on how you will get by on two-thirds of your salary for six months. Also, the more you know and the sooner you know it, the faster the application process can be. If you feel unemployment is imminent, it's worth checking the rules and resources with your human resources department and with your state unemployment office.

53. HEALTH INSURANCE PROTECTION: COBRA AND HIPAA

It's no news that the cost of health care has skyrocketed over recent years despite relatively tame inflation. There are many causes for this—administrative costs, technology, and the separation of consumer and payer (usually an insurance plan)—and it's too big a subject to tackle here. But when health care generates (or costs, depending on how you look at it) 17.6 percent of our GDP while manufacturing activities generate only 10 percent, something is off-center. Suffice it to say that the solution appears to be complex and far-off.

As a consumer, you will bear a greater burden for your health care costs. That's bad because you'll pay more. But in the bigger picture it may be good, because when you have to pay for something, you shop for the best value and hold providers accountable for what they deliver. That said, events that may severely affect your ability to get insurance coverage are out of your control—specifically, job changes and layoffs. If you are forced to transfer between states where an insurer may not provide benefits in both states, or you are forced to leave a job, your insurance coverage could be dropped "cold turkey," leaving you worse off, or forcing you to prolong an unfavorable situation just to keep the insurance.

Congress recognized that and passed two laws that can help: the Consolidated Omnibus Budget Reconciliation Act (COBRA) of 1985, and the Health Insurance Portability and Accountability Act (HIPAA) of 1996. These laws were intended to provide personal health care stability, and stability for the economy as a whole. Then, in 2010, Congress and the Obama administration passed the widely known and somewhat controversial Patient Protection and Affordable Care Act, commonly known as "Obamacare," (see #54 Obamacare) to deal with many of these issues, including availability to previously uninsurable individuals, and offering many other provisions to more widely mandate and reshape the availability of health coverage.

What You Should Know

Among other provisions, COBRA allows you as an eligible employee to keep your insurance for up to eighteen months after leaving a job (longer under some conditions, like disability). Now, "keep your insurance" doesn't mean that it's free—you'll have to pay the premium. But it does save you from having to prove eligibility or insurability, and it allows you to maintain coverage at the group rate provided to your employer.

While COBRA helps, in practice it was found that only a small minority of ex-employees actually take advantage of it for the full eighteen-month period, as most employees opt for lesser and cheaper coverage than paid for by the employer. But COBRA can help you bridge the gap until you find this cheaper option.

The HIPAA act, in practice, has been more about the rules of privacy and transfer of medical records and information. But one of the key provisions allowed employees to transfer from one job to another without requalifying for insurance; that is, a preexisting condition was not to be grounds for denying insurance at the new employer. There are some wrinkles if an employee moves to a new state where the old insurer doesn't do business, but in general, the law fixes what it intended to fix and, like COBRA, helps employees leave unwanted jobs.

Why You Should Care

Assuming you have health benefits with your job in the first place, if you have any inkling that your job might go away, or that it might be time for a change, it makes sense to learn about these two laws. Your health insurance provider or human resources department should be able to help you more.

54. OBAMACARE

"Obamacare" is the nickname given—mainly by opponents—to the landmark health care legislation more formally known as the Patient Protection and Affordable Care Act (PPACA) passed in March of 2010. The name "Obamacare" stuck after it was used and endorsed for use by the president himself.

What You Should Know

Obamacare, which had roots in some of the health care reform legislation attempted but not passed in the Clinton administration, brings sweeping changes to health care delivery and cost recovery over a period of eight years after its passage. The main intentions are to bring more affordable care to more people, and to increase access to certain segments of the population all but shut out of the current system. In numbers, the law intends to address the high cost of health care, currently consuming some 17.6 percent of GDP, and the estimated 45–50 million individuals not previously covered by health insurance or entitlements.

The primary mechanisms of Obamacare are:

- *Individual mandate.* Most individuals will be required to purchase health coverage (and certain employers with more than fifty employees to supply it), else be penalized for opting out. That mandate comes with subsidies to help out low-income individuals and families with incomes up to 400 percent of the federal poverty level (currently $11,170 for an individual and $23,050 for a family of four). Those subsidies are paid on a sliding scale depending on income level. The intent of this provision is to broaden coverage and bring more "healthy" people into the insurance pool, lowering the costs for everyone, at least in theory.

- *Guaranteed issue.* Health insurers will no longer (as of 2014) be able to deny coverage to anyone based on health, or cancel insurance for anyone who gets sick. No dollar limits can be applied to total lifetime coverage. Certain "essential" features like maternity coverage are compulsory, as are free preventive checkups after 2017.

- *Insurance exchanges.* States are mandated to operate, or have access to, health insurance exchanges for individuals to compare and buy insurance, and to enact income-based subsidies.

- *New taxes and cost savings measures.* To pay for subsidies, new and higher taxes are imposed on high earners for Medicare. Among the changes are a 2.3 percent excise tax imposed on medical equipment makers and importers, reduced tax benefits from medical expense deductions and flexible spending arrangements, reduced payments and increased audits of payments by Medicare to Medicare providers, and a "luxury tax" on so-called "gold-plated" health insurance benefits received by certain individuals (to take effect in 2018).

Why You Should Care

A major portion of Obamacare (individual mandate, subsidies, exchanges, and guaranteed issue) is set to take effect in 2014, so the long-term effects of this major policy change are yet to be felt. While more people will have access to coverage, and people will be less likely to be penalized for age or sickness, there is considerable concern that it will do little to reduce the overall cost of health care, except perhaps from some savings in Medicare costs (which may show up elsewhere as health providers "reallocate" costs). Higher demand from tens of millions more insured could drive health care prices higher. Additionally, if younger, healthier individuals choose to opt out of the individual mandate (by paying the penalty), the resulting insurance pools will be too small and overweighted with higher-cost, older, sicker individuals—and premiums will rise, not decrease as intended. Opponents of the legislation believe that driving costs down should have been first priority; if low enough, resulting insurance premiums would be more affordable, and people would subscribe naturally, without a mandate.

Whether you're covered by an employer, Medicare, or are an individual health coverage purchaser, you should watch which way the winds blow on this one. There could be a lot more changes as certain provisions start to take place.

CHAPTER 6

Economic Schools and Tools

Just as Democrats, Republicans, and others have different views on politics and public life, there are also different "parties" and schools of thought on economics and the economy. These schools of thought, like the political parties, have their leaders and their followers, and many of them, like "supply-side economics," work their way indelibly into the political vernacular.

Beyond such popular political panaceas, anybody who has spent time reading the papers or trying to understand this nebulous thing we call the economy has doubtless run into terms like "fiscal policy" and "Keynesian economics" and "monetary policy" and the "Chicago school." It's sophisticated stuff, most originating from the academic world, and hardly food for pleasant family dinner conversation, at least in most families.

But these schools of economic thought are interesting and important for anyone wishing to know how an economy works, and what "knobs and dials" can be used to control it. And the debate around which school works best or explains some kind of crisis can be interesting stuff—if you take it in small doses, like the summaries following. Otherwise, economic schools and their discussion can go into reams of articles and books and be about as dry as a southern Arizona zephyr.

Have no fear. As with other principles described in this book, the economic schools are presented on a "what you need to know" basis.

55. FISCAL POLICY

In the natural course of business and commerce, the economy may expand, contract, or linger in the doldrums, creating pleasure or pain for individuals, corporations, and society as a whole (see #8 Business Cycle). As a measured effort to provide some stability and reduce pain among certain individuals or sectors of the economy, governments try to influence the economy, and smooth out the down cycles in particular.

There are two primary ways the federal or any national government can influence the economy: *fiscal policy* and *monetary policy*. *Fiscal policy* is the use of government spending and tax policy (see #47 Tax Policy and Income Taxation) to put money into or take money out of the economy. Monetary policy (see #56), on the other hand, influences the economy through changes in the money supply and interest rates (see #17 Money Supply and #21 Interest Rates).

What You Should Know

By congressional design or approval, governments can change the level and direction of spending quickly. As a first step in the recovery plan for what turned out to be the Great Recession, Congress passed the American Recovery and Reinvestment Act of 2009, providing more than $700 billion in new, "shovel-ready" spending programs across the country. This is the largest and one of the most quickly passed fiscal stimulus packages in history.

Fiscal stimulus programs like this are designed to provide jobs and thus stimulate aggregate economic demand by giving earners the ability to spend more money. Some stimulus packages are also designed to help certain parts of the economy (as opposed to the whole), or to strengthen or encourage specific sectors. The 2009 stimulus package, for instance, contained spending for alternative energy technologies. Some fiscal stimulus programs can help reduce the effects of poverty or accomplish other social or distribution-of-income objectives.

Stimulus may also be accomplished by reducing taxes, as was done several times since the beginning of the Reagan administration in the early 1980s. The tax rebate checks sent to most Americans during 2008 and the 2 percent "holiday" on payroll taxes in effect for 2011 and 2012 were more recent examples.

Fiscal policy can also be used dampen or attenuate an economy. This can occur either by reducing spending (difficult to do politically in the short run) or by raising taxes.

Economists are somewhat split on the effectiveness of fiscal policies. As recently demonstrated, tax reductions and especially tax rebates during tough times can simply be used for saving and thus don't stimulate the economy (see #35 Paradox of Thrift). Government spending increases and decreases can be very political. They may not be allocated to the greatest need but rather subject to intense lobbying, resulting in waste and a significant loss of time before the benefits are realized (even the rapidly passed 2009 law wasn't expected to have real effect for as much as a year). For these reasons, many believe that monetary policy is more effective, but it has boundaries too. Notably, Congress controls fiscal policy while the Federal Reserve (see #30 Federal Reserve) controls monetary policy. Most likely, a combination of the two works best, as has been deployed over the course of time (see #57 Keynesian School and #58 Chicago School).

Why You Should Care

Government is in place to use your tax dollars to make your country a better place to live; fiscal policy is one of the biggest tools it has to do this. How the government spends money is important, as are the size and nature of the budget deficits that may result (see #42 Federal Deficits and Debt). Fiscal policies, especially those involving tax changes, are likely to affect you.

56. MONETARY POLICY

While fiscal policy moderates economic growth and stability directly through government spending and taxation, monetary policy does it a bit more indirectly by controlling the supply of money and its cost through interest rates.

What You Should Know

When there is more money in the system, in theory and usually in practice, there is more economic activity. People have more money to make purchases or to pay off debts to enable more purchases later. The Fed can put more money into the system directly or by reducing interest rates through open market operations (see #32 Fed Open Market Operations).

Adding money to the system usually has a fairly rapid effect, for it stimulates lending and also sets expectations of easier money down the road; business decision-makers have more dollars to chase both now and in the future. But putting more money in the economy to chase the same amount of goods and services, especially when the supply of certain key goods is constrained, as happened in the 2008 oil market, can be highly inflationary—those additional dollars make all dollars worth less.

Monetary policy also influences exchange rates (see #92 Currency Policy and Exchange Rates), which in turn can stimulate or attenuate an economy. Lower interest rates make the dollar relatively less attractive because foreign investors will receive less interest on their holdings. This drives down the value of the dollar against world currencies, which also stimulates U.S. demand as prices for American goods become relatively more attractive to overseas buyers.

Over time, monetary policy has received greater emphasis as a tool to regulate the economy. One big reason is that it works quickly and largely without congressional approval. Policymakers feel they've learned how to moderate the business cycle quickly and efficiently with it, and have learned how to adjust all the knobs and dials (not just interest rates) to achieve desired outcomes. The quantitative easing bond-buying programs of the past few years are an excellent example.

Critics feel the overuse of monetary stimulus has left the door open for serious inflation problems in the future as money supply increases have hit all-time records. Many now advocate slow and steady monetary growth—not harsh expansion and contraction cycles tied to big increases and decreases in the Fed funds rate—as the proper way to achieve economic prosperity and stability.

Why You Should Care

Monetary policy will affect your daily life. Most of the effect is indirect, via a healthy and more stable economy. If you're in the market for a mortgage or a short-term loan, monetary policy will have some effect on the interest rates you'll pay. Since monetary policy takes aim mostly at short-term interest rates, however, the effect on longer-term mortgage rates is not direct. Monetary policy will also affect the amount of interest you receive on savings. Finally, we all should be aware of the potential long-term effects of monetary growth on inflation (see #18 Inflation and #59 Austrian School).

57. KEYNESIAN SCHOOL

The Keynesian school, often referred to by other names like Keynesian economics or even the somewhat haughty "neoclassical synthesis," is a school of analysis and thought about the greater economic environment and the role that government should play in that environment. Essentially, the Keynesian school believes strongly in the theory and practice of capitalism but holds that government intervention, in several forms, is necessary to smooth the bumps and keep capitalist societies on a healthy, steady, and prosperous course.

What You Should Know

Keynesian economic theories went public during the Great Depression, and were the basis for British economist John Maynard Keynes's 1936 book *The General Theory of Employment, Interest and Money*. At that time, economists and policymakers were intent on finding causes and cures for the depression under way, which many attributed to a complete failure of the capitalist model. Keynes set out to prove that capitalism was okay, it just needed some government intervention occasionally, and that intervention should never be mistaken for government *control*—that is, a planned economy.

The Keynes view holds that without intervention, the economy will function, but not optimally. Businesses and business leaders can make suboptimal decisions based on incorrect perceptions or lack of information. This leads to underperformance, or in some cases "overperformance," a boom led by unrealistic expectations. These decisions and overreactions lead to suboptimal demand, loss of output, and unemployment, which of course then serve to make the situation worse. In this view, government policies, including fiscal and monetary stimulus, would be used to increase aggregate demand and economic activity. That stimulus would travel through the economy several times, creating a *multiplier* effect directly proportional to the *velocity* with which it traveled.

Monetary stimulus, to resolve the Great Depression at that time, would be accomplished through massive government investments and by lowered interest rates. Both were done, most particularly the government investments through WPA and other programs. Ironically, the theory was really proven effective by the economic boost given by World War II. Keynes also went against the grain in maintaining that deficits were okay, governments didn't need to balance budgets in the short run, and increased economic activity would fill budgetary gaps later. It should be noted that Keynes did not advocate deficit spending per se, but rather as a necessary investment to smooth economic cycles.

The details of the theory and the effects on wages, prices, and so forth are much more involved and complicated. Over time, U.S. government policy has embraced Keynesian economics, although elements of the Chicago school (or Monetarist school) are also deployed. The Austrian school, favoring little to no government intervention as a way to remove inefficiency more quickly, takes an opposing and intellectually enticing point of view. These are covered in the next two entries.

* deficit spending – spending funds usually in excess of amount of income, usually requiring borrowed dollars

Why You Should Care

In your normal life you won't be confronted with having to decide whether you're a Keynesian, or with the task of implementing Keynesian policy. But it's helpful to understand the underpinnings of government policy, and *why* the government does what it does. Those actions *do* affect you.

58. CHICAGO OR MONETARIST SCHOOL

While John Maynard Keynes favored government intervention to smooth supply and demand for goods and services as a way to achieve economic growth and stability (see #57 Keynesian School), another school of thought claimed that stability was a matter of equilibrium between supply and demand of *money*, not the goods and services themselves. This school of thought, largely held by members of the University of Chicago faculty, most notably Dr. Milton Friedman, is known as the Chicago or Monetarist school.

What You Should Know

Monetarism focuses on the macroeconomic effects of the supply of money, controlled by the central banks. Price stability is the goal, and policies like Keynesianism, which can lead to excessive monetary growth in the interest of stimulating the economy, are inherently inflationary.

Monetarists hold that authorities should focus exclusively on the money supply. Proper money supply policy leads to economic stability in the long run, at the possible expense of some short-term pain. Monetarists are more laissez-faire in their approach—that is, the economy is best left to its own actions and reactions. To the monetarist, money supply is more important than aggregate demand; the pure monetarist would increase money supply (in small, careful increments) to stimulate the economy rather than take more direct measures to stimulate aggregate demand. The Great Depression, in the Chicago school, was caused by a rapid contraction in money supply, brought on in part by the stock market crash, not a contraction in demand per se.

To the monetarists, the more direct approaches to stimulating aggregate demand are considered irrevocable (once the government intervenes, it is difficult to disengage). Worse, they crowd out private enterprise as government thirst for borrowed money to fund stimulus makes it harder and more expensive for the private sector to borrow. Monetarists also suggest that Keynesian stimulation changes only the timing and source but not the total amount of aggregate demand.

The monetarist point of view has always been embraced by policymakers who endorse a tight vigil over money supply in addition to more traditional fiscal stimulus and interest rate intervention. Fed Chairman Paul Volcker, and later Alan Greenspan, were monetarists, although critics are quick to point out that Greenspan got carried away and created too much growth in money supply, which led to strong boom and bust cycles in stocks and later in real estate. It did not lead to the expected inflation, thanks in part to the availability of inexpensive goods from Asia. We got lucky, but this attenuation of inflation may be unsustainable, particularly with the recent growth in money supply used to mitigate the Great Recession.

Why You Should Care

Unless you aspire toward a degree in economics, you don't need to be too familiar with the details of the Chicago school, nor its many proponents from the Windy City. The greater interest is in knowing where policy comes from and why.

59. AUSTRIAN SCHOOL

The Austrian school, while founded in Vienna long ago, has largely emigrated to the United States. One of its strongest proponents, Friedrich Hayek, a University of Chicago faculty member, popularized many of its teachings in the mid-twentieth century.

What You Should Know

The basic premise of the Austrian school is that human choices are subjective and too complex to model, and thus it makes no sense for a central authority to force economic outcomes. Like monetarism, but to a greater degree, it is a "laissez-faire" economic philosophy.

The Austrian school takes the contrarian view that most business cycles are the inevitable consequence of damaging and ineffective central bank policies. Government policies tend to keep interest rates too low for too long, creating too much credit and resulting in speculative economic bubbles and reduced savings. They upset a natural balance of consumption, saving, and investment, which, if left alone, would make the consequences of business cycles far less damaging.

The money supply expansion during a boom artificially stimulates borrowing, which seeks out diminishing or more far-fetched investment opportunities (like Florida real estate in 1925–1928 and again in 2005–2007), and more recently an outsized interest in high-yield bonds and other riskier fixed-income securities. This boom results in widespread "malinvestments," or mistakes, where capital is misallocated into areas that would not attract investment had the money supply remained stable.

When the credit creation cannot be sustained, the bubble bursts, asset prices fall, and we enter a recession or bust. If the economy is left to its natural path, the money supply then sharply contracts through the process of deleveraging (see #9 Deleveraging), where people change their minds and want to pay off debt and be in cash again. If governments and policy get involved to mitigate the pain of the bust by creating artificial stimulus, they delay the inevitable economic adjustments, making the pain last longer and setting us up for more difficulties later—harsher cycles and more inflation. Furthermore, so-called "creative destruction"—the weeding out of inefficient or uneconomical businesses and investments in favor of efficient ones—is delayed or avoided entirely, much to our long-term detriment.

The recent boom and subsequent Great Recession had many of the footprints of the Austrian scenario. A credit-stimulated over-expansion led to a bust; the government didn't know what to do about it; bad businesses and business models, like many banks, were propped up. In the Austrian school such businesses should be allowed to fail, for the economy will return to health more quickly, and a patient once on medicine will always require medicine.

Hayek himself criticized Keynesian policies as collectivist and never temporary. Perhaps Austrian school economist Joseph Schumpeter, who coined the term "creative destruction," summed up its point of view best in 1934: "Recovery is sound only if it does come of itself."

Why You Should Care
The Austrian school may seem radical, perhaps radically conservative, and almost antigovernment in nature. That said,

many of the symptoms proponents talk about, and much of their analysis of the Great Depression, resonates. It should help you maintain a healthy skepticism of government action, though most economists don't go this far in condemning the role of government. As an individual, it helps to have a balanced view of what's going on, and to understand the upsides and downsides of any government intervention. By the way, Austrian school disciple Murray Rothbard's *America's Great Depression, Sixth Edition* (CreateSpace Independent Publishing Platform, 2011) is a fascinating read if you enjoy this sort of thing.

60. SUPPLY-SIDE ECONOMICS

Capitalism is founded on the notion that people produce goods and services under their own free will, and that they earn the appropriate rewards for their achievement. Supply-side economics extends this fundamental school of thought by arguing that the best way to achieve economic growth is by maximizing the *incentive* to produce, or *supply* goods and services. That's best done by reducing taxes and regulation, allowing the greatest rewards, and allowing those goods to flow to market at the lowest possible prices.

What You Should Know

The term "supply-side economics" is relatively recent, coming into the language in the mid 1970s. Supply-side economics spawned close cousins in the form of "trickle-down economics" (see #61) and Reaganomics (see #62); all three members of this happy family got a good test in the 1980s in the administration of Ronald Reagan.

Supply-side economics attempts to optimize tax rates—that is, *marginal* tax rates, or rates paid on the highest dollar earned. The optimization is achieved by setting the tax rate low enough to avoid *discouraging* individual production and earning, but high enough to encourage *enough* production and earning to maximize total tax revenues. That in turn offsets the potential loss in tax revenue by lowering the tax rates. Stated differently, the tax rate matters more to individuals, total taxes collected matters more to government.

The relationship between tax rates and total tax revenue is illustrated in Figure 6.1. The Laffer Curve is named for economist Arthur Laffer, the supply-side proponent who created it.

Figure 6.1 Laffer Curve

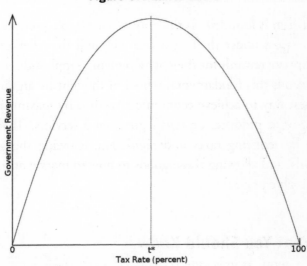

Source: Wikimedia commons, free license

The contrast between supply-side economics and other schools is illustrated by comparison with the Keynesian school, which contends that tax cuts should be used to create demand, not supply. The Keynesian school, by implication, would target the tax cuts toward lower-income earners who are most likely to spend, while the supply-sider would target them toward the higher-income earners, and especially business owners and leaders paying the highest tax rates. Doing so would stimulate the greatest increases in production; if these individuals faced 50 or even 70 percent tax rates, they would be less inclined to produce more and earn more (see #47 Tax Policy). The other end of the supply-side equation holds that the resulting economic growth from stimulated supply would make up for the loss in tax revenue.

The jury is still out on the effects of the supply-side "test" in the 1980s. Significant decreases in marginal tax rates were enacted and production did expand through the 1980s; the economy emerged from the Reagan administration far healthier than when he took office, even with the 1987 stock market crash. However, sufficient revenue was never generated to cover the tax decreases; the deficit grew persistently. That may have been caused more by increases in defense spending and other government programs than a failure in supply-side economics. Additionally, increased income inequality (the rich get richer, etc.) has also been a nagging criticism of supply-side policies.

More recently, supply-side economics has definitely been in the minds of the so-called "Tea Party" and other tax conservatives who believe even a slight increase (from 36 percent to 39.6 percent rates for top earners) tips the balance, but in effect through raises in Medicare taxes, capital gains taxes, and income taxes in many states, tax rates for the wealthy are going up anyway. Revenues have gone up considerably since the Great Recession, but still not enough to offset economic stimulus, spending increases, and growing entitlements (Social Security and Medicare). As such, the supply-side school has yet to fully prove itself, but there is a general feeling that things would be much worse if it had never come into play.

Why You Should Care

As an individual, particularly as an economically productive individual, you should favor the supply-side approach. It carries greater economic rewards for achievement, and makes hard work and investment more attractive. But before "buying" this approach from the politicians, make sure that the other end of the equation—government expenditures—are held in check. Otherwise, the additional tax revenues generated will not be sufficient and deficits will endure, putting America in a fundamental "box" of not being able to raise taxes if necessary. This mistake of the Reagan administration, and later the George H.W. Bush administration policy of "no new taxes," took a lot of wind out of the sails of this promising approach. We saw it again in the second Bush administration, and though attenuated somewhat under Obama, the general concept remains in play.

61. TRICKLE-DOWN ECONOMICS

The "trickle-down" school of economics carries a set of principles and actions very similar to supply-side economics (see #60), but the goal is different. While the supply-side school advocates stimulating production to benefit the economy as a whole and pay for the tax rate decreases that stimulated the production, the trickle-down school goes on to argue that increased production and wealth accumulated at the top will eventually "trickle down" to the masses.

What You Should Know

The premise is based on the idea that more prosperous business owners and leaders will produce more and take more risks, providing jobs and higher incomes for the masses. Additionally, the supply-side premise that greater production at a lower cost will lead to lower prices for consumers also suggests better standing for the lower economic tiers of society. Trickle-down economics takes the supply-side approach and extends it to a premise and promise of greater societal benefit for everyone.

The problem, of course, is that the wealth created at the top doesn't always trickle down so effectively. Many believe that quite the opposite happens—that the rich get richer, and not very much happens to anyone else. As William Jennings Bryan put it in the 1890s: "If you legislate to make the masses prosperous, their prosperity will find its way up through every class which rests upon them."

Indeed, the trickle-down theory was never directly advocated by the Reagan and Bush leadership, but was a constant theme in the congressional debates on tax policy, which went something like this: The wealthy will get what they want, the budget will be balanced on the back of higher tax revenues, and it will help the lower classes too. Unfortunately, the second two parts of the scenario never really played out—government spending exceeded the new revenues, and the wealthy chose to keep a lot of their wealth. By almost any measure, the wealthy got wealthier through the period. Why that happened is a matter of conjecture. First, lower tax rates and especially capital gains tax rates encouraged them to save it for themselves, not create new production and thus jobs; or second, in the face of an economy where considerable production was moving overseas, there wasn't enough job-creating activity to invest in.

Why You Should Care
Trickle-down economics, while attractive in principle, has still not met with measurable success in over 100 years of trying.

When politicians declare that making the rich richer will help everyone, take that with a grain of salt. That said, the supply-side foundation that the "trickle-down" outcome is based on shouldn't be dismissed as a bad idea.

62. REAGANOMICS

Reaganomics, the phrase coined for the economic policies of the Ronald Reagan 1981–88 presidency, was essentially an implementation of supply-side economics tailored for the times (see #60 Supply-Side Economics). The major premise and promise was an across-the-board reduction in income and capital gains tax rates to bolster an economy recovering from the stagflation hangover of the late 1970s (see #20 Stagflation).

What You Should Know
Ronald Reagan came into power in a particularly tricky economic period—one tricky enough that the traditional doses of monetary medicine would have made problems worse. The bulge in inflation in the late 1970s (see #18 Inflation) was caused by forces beyond monetary policy—that is, the supply shock and price escalation in the energy sector. Worse, inflation had become part of the daily mentality of consumers and business leaders alike; everyone expected it, and so raised prices defensively in advance of it. Inflation was a self-fulfilling prophecy.

The standard money-supply remedies for inflation were clearly not working. The Fed funds rate reached an all-time high in 1980 and led to the recession of 1981–82, but did not do as much to temper inflation or inflationary expectations as one would have hoped (see #21 Interest Rates). The challenge of the

Reagan administration was to combat inflation and stimulate growth *without* relying on traditional monetary policy.

The solution was a hybrid of monetary and supply-side economics. The Fed began lowering interest rates to increase money supply; at the same time, supply-side initiatives of lower taxes and promises of better times spurred production. The increased production then consumed, or "mopped up," the excess liquidity, or money, pumped into the economy. While more money chasing the same amount of goods and services leads to inflation, more money chasing *more* goods and services does not.

The Reagan administration, playing its "trickle-down economics" card to justify and pass the programs, used the expression "a rising tide lifts all boats" (see #61 Trickle-Down Economics). The economy rebounded while commodity prices fell at the same time—a rare combination that might be attributed to the combined policy. Detractors maintain that the high interest rates alone (they were declining, but still historically high—see Figure 3.1) brought the fall in commodity prices, but this argument seems out of place, because the economy was indeed rebounding.

Tax revenues—at least nominal, or not inflation-adjusted—grew. They fell as a percent of GDP, but that was intended and expected with lower tax rates. Real tax revenues did not increase, however, until 1987. It should also be noted that while federal income tax rates dropped, FICA taxes for Social Security and Medicare, as well as taxes in many states, increased.

Still, it looks like Reaganomics was indeed a dose of innovative medicine that worked for the most part. If it had been pulled off with a balanced budget, which did not happen, largely due to defense and certain other increases in expenditures, the case would be clear. A growing deficit stains the argument somewhat; one wonders what the economic outcome would have been without the additional government spending. Arguably, the Clinton years and the balanced budget they produced were more indicative of the benefits of Reaganomics than the Reagan years themselves.

Why You Should Care

The Reaganomics experience showed us all that creative approaches to solving economic problems and aiding prosperity can work. One should be concerned about budget deficits, but one should also not be led to think that tax increases are the best way to close budget gaps. The George W. Bush years (2001–2008) look more like reckless tax policy designed to favor the rich without hope of increasing revenues, and deficits increased widely while the seeds of the Great Recession—too much spending on overinflated assets, and a lax view of risk—were sown. The policies of the Obama administration haven't been able to touch the rich so much as the president himself would have liked, and new spending has dramatically increased deficits, but there is some evidence that tax revenues are increasing even without major tax rate changes, Perhaps in the next edition of this book we'll be able to say that Reaganomics and supply-side policies *really do* work, but for right now, the Reaganomics practiced during the Reagan administration appears to be a much more carefully considered experiment.

63. BEHAVIORAL ECONOMICS

What? You've got to be kidding. People don't follow the economic rules? People do things that don't fit neatly into demand and supply curves? People respond differently to different situations depending on stress, time, and what they see others around them doing?

You bet. And the presence of such "misbehavior" has given rise to a school of economics that combines economics with psychology, *behavioral economics*. This marriage of two subjects, both hard to research and quantify, has taken center stage in economic thought, as economists and policymakers struggle to fix and avoid economic problems.

What You Should Know

Behavioral economics applies social, cognitive, and emotional factors to better understand economic decisions by consumers, borrowers, and investors, and how they affect market prices and behavior. In short, it applies a human factor to decision making, a dose of "psychological realism." Behavioral economists try to figure out how and why actual behavior differs from rational and even selfish behavior—that is, the lowest cost, lowest risk, or most profitable course of action.

Interest in behavioral economics has increased as a result of the recent mortgage crisis and real estate bubble. Why did so many unsuspecting citizens take on so much debt, so much risk, and so much cost, assuming all along that the real estate market was foolproof? People have been asking such questions for years, dating back to the tulip bulb mania of the early 1600s. But it happens again and again through history. The answer seems to lie somewhere in the "madness of crowds," or the tendency for people to assume something is right because everyone else is doing it. Moreover, studies indicate that many people jump into these things because they fear being left out; *not* investing becomes the irrational decision.

In the fall of 2008, the U.S. economy went from an overdose of risk to complete risk avoidance in a matter of months. We went from lending 100 percent of value to a subprime customer to not lending anything at all.

Policymakers have begun to take such factors into account when making policy decisions—although they obviously have a way to go in truly understanding economic behavior, especially in crisis times.

Why You Should Care

Next time you think about "going along with the crowd," make sure you're acting in what economists would call "rational self-interest." Not all economic or financial decisions can be approached with rigid, mathematical, dollars-and-sense precision; surely your color preference in a car has little to no rational basis. That said, as an individual you are better off for the most part by adhering to economic reality. For society it's good to know that economists no longer assume that everybody is completely rational; that will lead to less costly policy and to fewer overcorrections in the business and boom-bust cycle. If you want to dig deeper, Dan Ariely's *Predictably Irrational: The Hidden Forces that Shape Our Decisions* (Harper Perennial, 2010) is a fascinating read on the subject.

64. NEW DEAL

At the height of the Great Depression, with unemployment rates exceeding 25 percent, a broken banking system, and rampant business failures, the newly elected President Franklin D. Roosevelt and his staff developed a complex set of economic programs to deal with these problems. In fact, he called the set of new programs and laws the "New Deal," and the name stuck. Until 2008, anyway, the New Deal was by far the largest coordinated government effort to deal with the effects of an economic bust;

the New Deal was broader in reach, if not as expensive as the economic stimulus and bank bailout programs recently undertaken.

What You Should Know

The programs and laws, largely initiated between 1933 and 1935, were aimed at providing economic relief for citizens, and particularly the unemployed, and with the reform of the business practices that gave rise to the bust in the first place. It was really a deal, as it traded off certain kinds of government spending in favor of other programs to revitalize the economy. A balanced budget was a goal, although many economists, particularly from the Keynesian school, maintain that it was a mistake to balance the budget in the depths of a depression.

Roosevelt, his Treasury secretary Henry Morgenthau Jr., and Congress started the New Deal by cutting government spending on military, the post office, general government salaries, and veterans' payments by a total of about $500 million (the total U.S. budget in 1933 was about $5 billion).

Employment relief came in the form of the Works Progress Administration (WPA) and similar agencies created to provide jobs building public buildings, parks, schools, and roads, which added numerous cultural assets to our landscape. Laws standardizing collective bargaining, providing minimum wages, and eliminating child labor were passed. Social Security (see #50) was part of the New Deal, as were other prominent economic institutions still in place today, such as the Federal Deposit Insurance Corporation (FDIC), the Federal Housing Administration (FHA), the Securities Acts of 1933 and 1934, the Securities and Exchange Commission (SEC), and government-sponsored lending enterprises like Fannie Mae.

The whole point was not just to stimulate the economy but also to provide a fair and predictable base within which it could move forward with a degree of confidence—public confidence as well as confidence between businesses, labor, and government. Many deride the New Deal as tending toward socialism, believing it has left too strong a legacy of government intervention and regulation. Others say the New Deal didn't go far enough, that it was too conservative, and that we were only bailed out of the Depression by the advent of World War II. What is certain is that the New Deal was enormous in scale and creatively constructed to solve a lot of problems and serve a lot of interests at once. Seldom if ever have we seen a government action or program with this much effect or historical significance.

Why You Should Care

Not only was the New Deal historically significant as a remedy for the Great Depression—it has also left a legacy of programs that are just as important to today's economy, if not more so, than they were at the time. The New Deal is also a model for economic remedies being attempted or discussed today, although today's remedies are larger in scale and less constrained by budgetary considerations.

65. PLANNED ECONOMY/SOCIALISM

Mention the idea of a planned economy to almost anyone and you're likely to get a look of concern in return. Yet during the Great Recession the federal government clearly got more involved in the day-to-day fortunes and operations of the economy—by necessity, some say, or by choice, as others complain.

So, what is a "planned economy," anyway? And do recent government interventions represent a brush with socialism?

What You Should Know

The various levels of "planned economy" that may occur in practice go from "least to most" in terms of planning and control:

- In a *planned market economy*, the state influences the economy through laws, taxes, subsidies, and outright infusions of cash, but does not force or compel economic outcomes. It is the "invisible hand" we all learned about in high school economics and has been more or less the state of American economics over the centuries.
- A *planned economy* is an economy in which the government, by edict, controls production, distribution, and prices. Governments don't own private entities, but they must comply with the plan and report all activity. While the U.S. government took control of the railroads briefly in World War I, this model has been more common in other countries, particularly in the Eastern Bloc, but also in places like China and India before relatively recent reforms.
- In a *command economy*, the government not only controls but also has substantial ownership of commerce and industry. One thinks of the current and former communist countries, but the model is common in Latin America; Venezuela and Cuba are examples.

Socialism does not fit neatly in this continuum but is regarded as having the broader political and socioeconomic objective of equalizing the distribution of wealth and income. That is accomplished through the means of direct income redistribution policies, central economic planning, and ownership or the formation of cooperatives. The state plans or controls the means of production toward achieving the egalitarian objective.

The interesting debate today is to what degree government actions in the wake of the Great Recession represent a move toward more of a planned economy. Economist and investment company manager Axel Merk, in his book *Sustainable Wealth* (Wiley, 2009), put it thus:

> More than most other world nations, the United States has "walked the walk" of capitalist freedom and self-determinism, although policy at its highest levels has acted as an "invisible hand" and to "lean against the wind" to move toward politically acceptable economic outcomes. But in the aftermath of the credit crisis that hand has started to become more visible. The fear is, of course, that once that process gets started, once trust is replaced by government intervention, it can spin out of control; the world has ample experience with the iron hands of socialism and communism.
>
> As the credit crisis was dealt with, major sectors of the economy—the financial industry, the auto industry—effectively became wards of the state. They became dependent on the U.S. government for financial sustenance and even for leadership through the crisis. The state went further into the private economy by granting credit to specific industries and businesses, something which had almost never happened before, certainly not on such a large scale, in U.S. history. It was, in short, a brush with a planned economy.

Merk goes on to argue that a severe recession "ought to be the lesser evil than a planned economy," and while we are still a far cry from communism, we "must keep our eyes open and not be blinded by the perceived 'help' of money printed by the Fed."

Why You Should Care

It's important to understand today's economic actions and reactions, and those observed before, during, and after the Great

Recession, in the context of government influence and control. Whatever your philosophy and acceptance or rejection of this intervention, you should understand how it fits into the greater context.

CHAPTER 7

Finance and Financial Markets

Most of what we've talked about is the "macro" sector of the economy, the big picture, the government and its role, the greater economy in which we all participate. While these macro pieces provide the economic framework to produce the goods and services—the food, cars, and wine—you choose to consume, our capitalist system also requires private enterprise.

Private enterprise produces the goods and services we all want, and hires the majority of us as labor to produce those goods and services. It also depends on capital we supply as savings and investments. But the allocation of labor and especially capital between millions of households and hundreds of thousands of private-sector businesses is a vastly complex enterprise. The need to move money around to the right places gives rise to the financial markets and the financial services industry.

The history of the financial markets and the financial services industry is full of success and failure, and as we emerge from the Great Recession, the pendulum has clearly swung from success to failure and back in the direction of success. The financial services industry grew beyond its traditional role as facilitator of the public and private economy into a large part of the economy in and of itself. Newfangled financial instruments and an excessive liberalization of credit served to fill the coffers of the industry to the point where in 2005 the industry made some 40 percent of all profits made by America's top corporations. This distortion came home to roost in a big way when the resulting real estate bubble popped. It's enough to make you or anyone else mad, but that energy would be better spent understanding what happened, why, and what should be done to prevent a repeat performance.

As we move forward, the financial industry has retrenched, and new regulation, such as the Dodd-Frank Wall Street Reform and Consumer Protection Act of 2010 (see #39) will likely serve to curb the excesses of the past. That said, most of the markets and instruments of the financial services industry will continue to exist and play an important part in capital allocation and economic growth. What follows takes a look at these important private-sector building blocks of the economy.

66. DERIVATIVES AND DERIVATIVE TRADING

Anybody who's read even the slightest bit of economic or financial news in the past couple of years has run across the term *derivative*. Derivatives have been in the news a lot ever since the early days of the 2008–2009 financial crisis.

So what is a derivative, anyway? Simply, it's a financial contract or asset whose price is determined by the price of something else. Want to buy a thousand barrels of oil as an investment, or to use in your business, or to resell? You can, but you'd have to pay the full price for the oil, perhaps $100,000, and you'd have to find a place to store it. As an alternative, you can buy a derivative based on the price of oil, perhaps a futures contract, specifying delivery of that oil at a future date at a specified price. If the price of oil goes up, the price of your derivative will go up too.

What You Should Know

Derivatives can be based on almost any kind of underlying asset—a physical asset like a commodity, a financial asset like a stock or mortgage or bond or some other debt security, an index like a stock or interest rate or exchange rate index, or just about anything.

There are three primary types of derivatives:

- *Futures* specify the delivery of a fixed amount of something at an established date. Futures are traded on agricultural products, energy, metal, stock indexes, interest rates, currencies, and an assortment of other assets on futures exchanges, and represent relatively large bets on these items (see #80 Commodities, Futures, and Futures Markets). Note that you don't have to (and most people don't) wait for the expiration of a futures contract to settle; you can sell or buy it prior to that date based on market prices at the time.

- *Options* are contracts giving the right, but not the obligation, to buy or sell something on or before a future date, usually a stock, but sometimes a futures contract. Equity options are traded on thousands of stocks, and can also be traded on futures contracts; options are relatively smaller investments in size or total outlay, but can be very highly *leveraged* for large gains (the concept of leverage is described below).

- *Swaps* are a contract to exchange cash on or before a specified date based on the price of a particular asset. They differ from futures in that you don't actually buy the item; it is a contract simply to settle with cash on or before the settlement date. Additionally, swaps are more of a "one-off" contract custom-made between private parties; they're not traded as established securities available to the public on a securities exchange. A "credit default swap," which guarantees payment only in case of a credit default, is a bit different (see #69 Credit Default Swap).

Derivatives can be used to *hedge* or to *speculate*. Farmers will hedge against the decline in the price of wheat, for example, by *selling* a futures contract on what they are producing. That allows them to pocket some cash now, giving some insurance against a price fall, or even a crop failure. On the other side of the trade, a brewery might hedge by buying a futures contract to protect against price increases, or even to guarantee supply in times of shortage.

As a tool to speculate, investors not in the brewing or farming business may also "play" the wheat futures market, betting on a rise or decline in wheat prices based on a host of factors. Derivatives offer *leverage*. Leverage allows you to enjoy the price gains or suffer the declines of the underlying asset with as little as 5 or 10 percent of the value invested, a key attraction for speculators. You can buy that interest in $100,000 of oil for a tenth of that, but if it goes down, you'll lose your entire investment, and sometimes more.

Aside from helping farmers and brewers, the existence of derivatives gives investors and financial institutions ways to invest in things, and ways to manage risks. They also help bring more participants to any given market, making that market and its prices more truly reflect supply and demand. However, the broad array of derivatives and the opaque nature of some of the customized derivatives created through "financial engineering" in the last decade have caused considerable trouble. Additionally, derivatives traders overplayed their hands, writing more contracts than they could possibly cover. Forthcoming regulation will likely standardize trading and trading rules for some of the exotic derivatives, particularly swaps (see #69 Credit Default Swap). This will give a more favorable name to these instruments and help them move away from the "financial weapons of mass destruction" moniker assigned by billionaire investor Warren Buffett in 2002.

The size of the world derivatives market is phenomenal, estimated at some $1,200 *trillion* face or nominal value (although some estimates claim it to be higher). To put that figure in perspective, it is about twenty times the size of the entire global economy.

Why You Should Care

With so much bad news circulating about derivatives, it's a good idea to understand what they are, and know how they can cause trouble. That said, certain derivatives like stock options can actually be used to reduce your risk—that is, to hedge on your stocks. That can make a lot of sense for ordinary investors who know what they're doing.

67. ASSET-BACKED SECURITY

Asset-backed securities (ABSs) were once a dark corner of the financial world, a financial tool most people wouldn't commonly know or care about. But the 2008–2009 financial crisis put ABSs center stage, particularly the real estate versions known as mortgage-backed securities (MBSs) and so-called collateralized debt obligations (CDOs) (see #68). For the most part, ABSs aren't consumer products—they are bought and sold by large financial institutions—but in the interest of understanding the financial news, and understanding how "engineered" financial products like this can affect you, read on.

What You Should Know

An asset-backed security is a specially created financial instrument, or security, custom-built upon a pool of underlying assets. Those assets serve as collateral, and the income they generate is passed on to the ABS holder. Individually, the assets contained in the ABS, like mortgages or car loans, are small and difficult to sell in the open market. The ABS is designed to package them into a single, larger security so they are large enough to interest institutional investors, and if packaged clearly and carefully, to spread risk. If one asset in the portfolio fails, it will be only a small fraction of the portfolio. ABSs were created out of mortgages, car loans, credit card financing, and commercial loans and leases.

ABSs played a key role in the mortgage crisis. To lend more money on mortgages, banks engaged in the mortgage market learned to package mortgages into ABSs (or MBSs) and sell them as a package. The process is known as *securitization*—the offering institution created a security out of a number of individual assets. This accomplished two things: first, it helped the banks get funding for the loans, and second, it transferred the risk of default to the buyer. Investment banks and institutional investors (see #28 Investment Bank and #75 Institutional Investors) bought these securities because it was a handy way to tap into the mortgage market and chase higher returns than currently offered by the bond market or other fixed-income securities.

Prior to the crisis, as it turns out, the idea of ABSs caught on rapidly as a way to expand the mortgage market and lend into the real estate boom. In fact, this helped *cause* the boom, because it became easier to get funds to lend. Unfortunately, the buyers of ABSs did not fully understand the underlying risks in these securities; neither they nor the ratings agencies (see #77 Credit Rating Agency) factored in the notion that real estate prices might decline, and didn't perform a "due diligence" on the credit risk of assets that lay beneath the covers of the ABS. The result was a collapse in the value of ABSs held on bank and institutional books, and that as much as anything else led to the banking crisis. This was made worse by the fact that all ABSs are unique. Each is constructed on a specific batch of assets; no two are alike, so there is no market to value them, and little "transparency" as to their true worth.

Why You Should Care

The expansion of asset-backed securities led to "easier" lending terms, but also ultimately led to the financial crisis when the tide washed out on underlying asset values. The 2008 banking crisis led to a severe contraction in asset-backed security markets, which in turn caused a severe contraction in credit extended to businesses and consumers. It's a big part of why it got very difficult to get a loan during that period. Today, the ABS market has loosened somewhat, but tighter standards for underlying asset quality, necessary to make the markets work, has caused it to remain somewhat difficult to borrow if you have bad credit—and that's a good thing. Bottom line: ABSs are not necessarily a bad thing if risks are properly assessed. There is also a well-placed call to standardize ABSs and create more liquid, transparent markets to trade them.

68. COLLATERALIZED DEBT OBLIGATION (CDO)

Collateralized debt obligations are a form of ABS (see #67 Asset-Backed Security) that might be analogous to a stealth fighter jet compared to a small Cessna prop job. They are highly engineered, highly customized, securitized assets based on fixed-income securities, with mortgages again taking center stage in the recent boom.

What You Should Know

For the average consumer, CDOs are one of those topics that the more you know, the more you don't know. As it turns out, that phrase also applied to many in the financial world who didn't really understand nor could properly value the CDOs they bought and sold, and we now know the result.

Like ABSs in general, CDOs are carefully created packages containing underlying securities. A financial institution, and most likely a "special purpose entity" residing off the books of a major financial institution like an investment bank, would package a series of underlying assets into a security. These assets could be individual loans and mortgages, or they could be other ABSs. They were often called "structured investment vehicles." But it would be too simple to stop there. The CDO was then divided into segments, or "tranches," according to risk and rank of underlying assets, and these assets could be sold individually to other buyers. It gets worse—there were "synthetic" CDOs, "market value" CDOs, "arbitrage" CDOs, and "hybrid" CDOs; the financial engineering details are beyond the scope of this discussion.

The now-defunct Drexel Burnham Lambert engineered the first CDOs in the late 1980s. The market grew furiously in 2004–2006 as CDOs became the favorite tool to resell and transfer the risk of real estate mortgages. Buyers of CDOs included commercial and investment banks, pension funds, mutual funds, and other institutional investors seeking higher returns, which ranged from 2 to 3 percent higher than corporate bond rates at the time. Suffice it to say that, due to the complexity of these products, buyers often did not know what they were really getting.

The boom in CDOs is made clear by the statistics. In 2004 some $157 billion in CDOs were sold; that figure rose to $272 billion in 2005, $521 billion in 2006, $482 billion in 2007—then dropped to $56 billion in 2008 as the market came to appreciate the risks and complexities of these securities. It has remained somewhere near that size.

The lucrative fees paid to the creators of these securities helped lead to the boom and subsequent downfall. Investment banks and individual investment bankers made millions capturing their percentages of these securities as they were sold; the incentive was to build them as big, and sell them as fast, as possible. Those who created these products simply passed on their risks, which now have ultimately been borne or at least backstopped by the taxpayers. Now that these characteristics have come to light, it is likely that CDOs will continue to exist, but in a more transparent, standardized, and regulated form.

Why You Should Care

You'll never be approached to buy a CDO, but it's good to know what goes on in the world of high finance. Once the fallout from the credit crisis becomes clear and turns into appropriate regulation, transparency, and controls, CDOs should continue to be with us, although not at "boom" volumes, and their existence will help make credit more available to all of us.

69. CREDIT DEFAULT SWAP (CDS)

There are CDOs, CDSs, ABSs, MBSs, and more. The three-letter alphabet soup of high finance reached all-time proportions in the middle part of the first decade of the twenty-first century. It became hard to keep track of what these new innovations were, how they worked, and how they led to the financial downfall at the end of the decade. It's especially easy to assume that CDOs and CDSs—*credit default swaps*—were much the same thing, but in fact they were quite different. We examined CDOs in the previous entry; now it's time to move on to CDSs.

What You Should Know

A credit default swap is a special kind of derivative contract (see #66 Derivatives and Derivative Trading) in which the buyer pays a sum, known as a *spread,* for a contract specifying that if a certain company defaults on a credit instrument, like a bond or loan, the buyer gets a payoff. For example, a buyer might pay a spread of $50,000 to $100,000 for $10 or $20 million of default coverage. If this sounds like insurance, it is, and as a legitimate financial product, CDSs help bond buyers insure their risk.

Like insurance, CDS contracts were custom-written for the situation; they were not set up as standardized, market-tradable securities. And like insurance, most CDSs were developed and marketed by insurance companies. But unlike insurance, CDSs do not require the buyer to have an *insurable interest*—that is, a stake in the matter being insured. You can't buy life insurance on your next-door neighbor, but you can buy a few million in CDSs on company XYZ without owning any bonds or stock in that company whatsoever.

Because buyers of CDSs did not have to have an insurable interest, CDSs were used as a tool to speculate on the demise of companies. At the same time, in a manner similar to CDOs, financial companies and the individuals who work for them make huge commissions and bonuses for developing and selling CDSs. Hedge funds, among other large investors looking to boost returns, bought CDSs. Also, insurers like AIG looked at them as a way to generate relatively low-risk cash by collecting spreads against what were felt to be highly unlikely defaults. This turned out to be a dangerous combination—a handful of employees in a UK branch of AIG sold CDSs with a face value more than twice the value of the entire company, and we now know where that led.

Making matters worse was the fact that many CDSs were written not just to protect against default, but against the change in a credit rating or any other change in a company's financial condition. These triggers, to the surprise of most involved, were hit far more often during the financial crisis than anyone anticipated. CDSs were the primary factor in the $180 billion federal bailout of AIG.

JPMorgan Chase created CDSs in 1997; the face value of assets insured grew to some $45 *trillion* by 2007. Their spreads became a de facto indicator of a company's financial strength—or weakness; it was the rise in CDS spreads for Bear Stearns in early 2008 that spooked the credit markets, starved the company of credit, and led to its forced sale to—ironically—JPMorgan Chase. Today, financial regulators recognize the need for CDSs to provide the insurance intended, but are examining ways to regulate the market, including standardization of contracts and trading on an open and more visible exchange.

Why You Should Care

Like CDOs and most other asset-backed securities, you probably won't receive any offers to buy CDSs in your mailbox. But it's important to know where our financial system troubles came from, and to know that even the best and brightest of our insurance companies got caught with their hands in the proverbial cookie jar. Most likely the lessons have been learned, but if you hear of heavy CDS activity from an insurance or financial services company you're dealing with, look out.

70. MUTUAL FUND

You may have money to invest and you want to participate in the American economy, or perhaps other economies beyond American shores. But you don't have millions; more importantly, you don't have the expertise, the time, or the interest in becoming your own investment adviser. You just want to throw that job over the wall to someone else, and you're happy to pay a small fee for the privilege.

That's where mutual funds come into play for the typical consumer-investor today. Mutual funds are a popular vehicle for the investment of individual wealth, and have become a standard for investing retirement wealth, particularly the assets of 401(k)plans and other employer-sponsored retirement plans. Whether you intended to or not, you probably own a mutual fund somewhere, somehow.

What You Should Know

Mutual funds are the predominant form of what's known as an *investment company*. Investment companies are investment pools designed to achieve certain investing objectives, usually to capitalize on growth, income, or some combination of the two. They were chartered under and are governed by the Investment Company Act of 1940. The act is very specific about how investors are treated, how the fund discloses results, and how investors are paid by these funds. Compliance is strong, because the act is actively enforced by the SEC (see #44). There are about 14,000 mutual funds in existence today, and they have become a mainstay of Main Street, especially for retirement plan investing (see #51 Retirement Plans).

If you're a typical retail investor, you'll probably have to settle for the fairly ordinary returns these funds generate. They're largely safe, but tend not to outperform the market. They diversify your holdings, they're convenient, and they save you a lot of time. They work well when you have modest amounts, say $50,000 or less, to invest. And they're clearly better than not knowing what you're doing and getting stuck with the wrong individual stock investments—like Enron, AIG, or Washington Mutual, for instance.

With mutual funds, you do indeed pay for their services. Management and marketing fees can be typically 0.5 percent to 1.5 percent of your investment balance—whether or not your investment does well. If you lose 20 percent along with the markets, you still pay the fee, albeit on a smaller balance. Mutual funds also may create tax surprises if held in *taxable* (that is, nonretirement) investment accounts. Each year they buy and sell stocks, and if there are gains, you pay taxes on those gains. Since the fund share price is based on the "net asset value" of all securities in the portfolio, if you buy shares late in the year after a good market run, you will pay a higher price for the shares—and pay taxes on the capital gains that the previous owner realized when selling you the shares! Thus, it's better to buy mutual funds in the beginning of the year, and to do some research on the so-called *tax efficiency* of the fund—that is, whether they take shareholder tax considerations into account when buying and selling shares. Again, this is only for mutual funds not held in a tax-deferred retirement account—an IRA, 401(k), or some such.

Why You Should Care

Mutual funds are a good way for an individual investor to gain exposure to stocks, and to invest in challenging sectors of the market, like international stocks. Mutual funds make it much easier for the typical consumer to invest, and, along with the growth of individually directed and employer retirement plans, have indeed raised the share ownership among U.S. households from 10 percent or so in the 1960s to some 65 percent in 2007, but it has fallen off a bit to 54 percent in the wake of the Great Recession. Still, the high percentage of stock ownership is a good thing in terms of making capital available for businesses, and for allowing the ordinary individual to participate in prosperity. So far as mutual funds are concerned, like any product you buy, you should know what you gain and what you give up by investing in a given fund.

71. EXCHANGE-TRADED FUND (ETF)

Exchange-traded funds are an increasingly important and relatively new investment "product" designed, like mutual funds, to give you an easy, "prepackaged" way to participate in the world economy or certain segments thereof. Exchange-traded funds are closely related to mutual funds, but there are important differences. The first widely available ETF, the SPDR S&P 500 ETF Trust, commonly known as the "SPDR," released in January 1993. Since then, about 1,400 new funds have entered the fray, with some $1.6 trillion in assets—a large sum, but still only about a tenth of what's invested in the traditional mutual fund universe.

What You Should Know

Exchange-traded funds are pretty much what the name implies. Like mutual funds, they are groups or "pools" of investments that you can buy a share of for yourself. Unlike traditional mutual funds, their shares trade on exchanges, like the NYSE Arca electronic exchange. As such, the prices fluctuate throughout the day, and you can buy and sell them like any individual stock. So if you decide that agriculture is your thing but don't begin to know which company to invest in, you can simply buy shares of the Market Vectors Agribusiness ETF (ticker symbol "MOO") and let your investment harvest a few bushels of cash for you.

The 1,400 or so ETFs available cover a wide variety of market segments; you can invest in anything from agriculture to European stocks to bonds to physical gold to certain baskets of commodities priced in Australian dollars. Most ETFs own individual stocks, but some may own physical commodities or futures contracts for those commodities. ETFs can be grouped into General Equity (like the "SPDR" mentioned at the outset), International Equity, Dividend, Fixed-Income (mostly bonds), Commodity, Strategy (for example, low-volatility investments or companies that buy back their own shares), and Sector (companies in certain industries, like auto manufacturing).

Most ETFs are tied to specially created indexes; that is, rather than being actively managed by a fund manager (a professional human), they are simply modeled after a pre-existing index, like the S&P 500 indexes mentioned in the SPDR example. Financial firms have created indexes for almost anything; the index determines what investments are owned, and in what proportion. The ETF manager simply buys and sells securities in the open market to track the index. There are more than a dozen financial services firms offering ETFs to the public; the three largest and best known are BlackRock (branded "iShares"), Invesco ("Power-Shares"), and State Street Global Advisors ("SPDRs," now an entire family of funds).

ETFs offer several advantages to investors:

- *Low cost.* Fees and expenses are typically half of traditional mutual funds.
- *Convenience.* It's easy to buy, sell, and rotate these funds during the day, and to own as many or as few as you want at any time. ETFs cover wide or narrow swaths of the

market, making it easy to participate, say, in the economies of Eastern Europe, without becoming an expert or trading those securities directly.

- *Transparency.* It's easy to see and track what they own—that is, what *you* own.

Why You Should Care

ETFs are easy for individual investors, and offer a low-cost way to participate in the segments of the market best for you. They're easy to use and an excellent and relatively safe way to diversify. For the economy as a whole, they provide a low-cost and lower-risk opportunity for many more investors to invest and participate. Availability and use of ETFs in employer retirement plans (like 401(k)s) is growing, so you're more likely to run across them as investment choices if you haven't already. But because it is so easy to rotate, they can cause faster swings in the markets and between different sectors of the market—in short and to a degree, ETFs "speed" change in the markets.

72. HEDGE FUND

Suppose you're fortunate to have a great deal of "investable wealth." A million or more, tens of millions, even better. You aren't content to just perform with the market. And picking individual stocks and managing your own investments just isn't your thing. You want to be "in" with the big boys, scoring way better than average returns. You want 10, 15, or 20 percent or more, rather than the 5 percent everyone else is settling for. You want to invest the way other rich, famous, and privileged people do. A hedge fund might be your answer.

What You Should Know

As it turns out, hedge funds are the privileged-class answer to the ordinary mutual fund. In the interest of not meddling too much in the world of private wealth and capital, the 1940 act has two commonly used exemptions excluding certain types of funds from close regulation. These exemptions gave rise to what are now known as "hedge funds." As a result, hedge fund governance is limited primarily to two areas: who can invest and how they're sold. The early hedge funds did what the name suggests—they helped investors "hedge" against market downturns or other unforeseen events, because rules and predominant investing strategies made it difficult for ordinary funds or individual investors to do so.

There are two types of funds that exist under these relatively light rules. One type of fund is limited to 100 or fewer investors, and can only be marketed to investors with more than $1 million in investable assets, or verifiable income exceeding $200,000 a year. The other can have an unlimited number of investors, but each must have $5 million of investable assets. The first type doesn't have to be registered with the SEC at all, the second only if it has more than 499 investors. Furthermore, there's no requirement for the managers of either type of fund to be registered or otherwise qualified or credentialed with the SEC, or with any other regulatory body or trade organization. For most of their existence, the rules stated that neither type of fund could be "offered or advertised to the general public," but that rule was overturned in mid-2013 by the SEC, and advertisements will be permitted going forward.

As a result, hedge funds are largely left to do what they want, and the managers can charge some pretty hefty fees for their services. Common was the "2 and 20" compensation rule, where the manager is guaranteed a fee of 2 percent of the fund's net asset value plus 20 percent of the investment gains over a specified amount. That's a pretty powerful incentive.

Without close regulation, hedge funds are allowed to sell short, borrow money, and invest in "derivative" instruments like futures and options to enhance returns. Effectively, they can leverage their portfolio, controlling, say, $10 million in assets with, say, $2 to $5 million in equity. That's great when things are good, not so great when things go bad. Bottom line: hedge funds allow wealthy investors to chase high returns using exclusive private investments administered by managers with few boundaries, who tend to chase the highest returns possible to get the biggest fees. It's a potent combination for success, but also for failure.

Why You Should Care

Despite some of the horrendous losses incurred by some hedge funds in the Great Recession, not all hedge funds are bad, and they do bring a lot of capital to market from the coffers of the wealthy. However, their power and numbers, some 10,000 funds managing some $2.5 trillion in assets, can cause some pretty outsized market moves and distortions, such as the oil price run-up in mid-2008. When markets do well, most hedge funds do well—and vice versa. When things start turning south for hedge funds, because of leverage they're often forced to dump conservative investments, a factor that probably amplified the 2008–2009 stock and commodity market collapse.

Legislative attempts have been made to regulate hedge funds, and the 2010 Dodd-Frank Act (see #39) started to require managers of larger hedge funds with more than $150 million in assets and/or more than fifteen clients to be registered as Registered Investment Advisers, but not much else has happened in terms of regulatory oversight; hedge funds are still mainly in the "Wild West" corner of the investment markets.

73. PRIVATE EQUITY

Private equity is a general term for equity, or stock investments in businesses not traded on a stock exchange. Private equity is an important source of investment capital for distressed firms or brand-new companies, because they don't have to go through the rigors of public listing, accountability, and disclosure. *Venture capital*, investments made in new business ventures, is one form of private equity.

What You Should Know

Private equity companies can be firms or funds that typically get their money to invest from large institutional investors or very wealthy individuals, and in turn make investments in or acquire companies outright. Private equity firms may acquire already existing "public" companies or the majority of a company through leveraged buyouts (see #74), and usually use venture capital to take a smaller stake in order to minimize their risk.

For sure, private equity firms and their investors don't make their investments out of the goodness of their hearts; they are looking for a return, typically a substantial one, on their investments. If they simply wanted stock market or fixed-income returns, they would invest in stocks or fixed-income securities. Most private equity deals, including venture capital deals, seek to earn a large return, either by harvesting profits from the companies they invest in, or by selling them at a better price at maturity or after a turnaround.

Private equity was made famous by the many so-called "corporate raiders" who emerged in the 1980s—Carl Icahn, T. Boone Pickens, Kirk Kerkorian, Saul Steinberg, and others. These investors would buy large stakes of a company, in some cases enough to get themselves or their own people on the board of directors, and push for change. If successful, and especially if they employed leverage by borrowing to help finance their purchase, they reaped enormous profits. But that strategy didn't always work, as shown by the recent experience of Cerberus Capital Management, which bought Chrysler out of the Daimler-Chrysler merger only to put it into bankruptcy shortly afterward. More recently, Michael Dell teamed up with private equity investor Silver Lake Partners and certain other investors, including Microsoft, to buy Dell and take it private—such transactions and attempted transactions are not infrequent. Beyond Cerberus and Silver Lake, some of the larger names you'll read about in the private equity space today include Kohlberg Kravis Roberts (KKR), Bain Capital, Warburg Pincus, the Carlyle Group, and the Blackstone Group.

Why You Should Care

Private equity is important—and has become more important— as a source of corporate capital over the years. More often than not a company that "goes public"—starts selling shares to the public to trade on a stock exchange—has gone through a considerable incubation in the hands of private equity. You should know that when that firm goes public, it's a sign that the private equity firm has maximized its return on investment—which may not bode well for the company's immediate future. Also, while private equity serves a useful purpose in rescuing failing companies (when successful), when that company is taken public again, it may not be the best time to buy. Finally, there have been some cases where firms have been bought strictly for the short-term gain of the individual or private equity firm, then plundered for their cash and assets. Watch carefully if you invest in—or work for—one of these firms.

74. LEVERAGED BUYOUT (LBO)

Want to sound suave and sophisticated at a cocktail party when the subject comes around to finance? Just mention the words "leveraged buyout." A leveraged buyout is simply the purchase of a company by another company using "leverage," or borrowed money.

What You Should Know

The acquiring company may be a company in the same industry, or it may be a conglomerate or holding company (like Warren Buffett's Berkshire Hathaway), or a private equity firm specializing in LBOs. The borrowed money may come from traditional sources like banks or investment partnerships. Sometimes at least some of the money may come from the cash coffers of the company being acquired, and sometimes it may come from selling off some of the acquired company's assets. Finally, the acquired company's assets may be used as collateral on any debt issued to make the transaction. In some cases, an investment bank (see #28) might put together a consortium of lenders. Typically the debt ranges from 60 to 90 percent of the purchase price, and any debt issued in an LBO is considered high risk.

LBOs are more likely to be used when the acquired company has significant cash, stable cash flows, or quality "hard" assets that can be sold or used as loan collateral. Acquiring firms are often looking for good corporate assets in need of a turnaround, new management, or other operational improvements.

LBOs hit their stride in the 1980s, culminating with the $31 billion buyout of RJR Nabisco by LBO specialist KKR in 1989. The next big wave of LBOs hit during the 2005–2007 boom, with such names as Equity Office, Hertz, and Toys"R"Us being "taken out" by various acquirers.

More recently, leveraged buyout activity continues at a brisk pace because of relatively cheap borrowing rates, but no real big names have been "taken out." Some have involved major parts of companies, such as a recent $4.8 billion buyout of DuPont's auto paint business by the Carlyle Group.

Why You Should Care

LBOs have changed the corporate landscape, affording more companies more power to make more acquisitions, and cleaning the corporate "forest floor" of some companies past their prime. If you work for a company that is a target of an LBO, watch out; the acquiring company may look to streamline and trim assets (including you).

75. INSTITUTIONAL INVESTORS

Institutional investors are large organizations, public or private, that amass funds for an assortment of purposes and invest them in the markets. Their objective in most cases is to invest money on behalf of others, and their success is determined by market performance.

What You Should Know

The importance of institutional investors becomes clear when looking at some of the different types of institutions:

- *Pension funds* are among the largest and most influential groups of institutional investors. Not surprisingly, their objective is to build assets to fund retirements of private and public employees, although today more private retirement savings plans (see #51 Retirement Plans) are self-directed, like 401(k) plans, and are thus more likely to come into the markets via mutual funds. In 2012, total worldwide pension fund holdings were estimated at $30 trillion, with 79 percent of that in the United States, the United Kingdom, and Japan.

- *Mutual funds* are investment companies that invest on behalf of individual investors (see #70). Worldwide mutual fund assets totaled about $17 trillion in 2010.
- *Insurance companies* invest assets—collected premiums—in the markets to achieve growth, pay insurance claims, and ultimately (if things go right) reduce the premiums. Insurance company investments are typically fairly stable, but in the wake of major disasters, insurance companies may sell sizable chunks of assets to pay claims, which can cause some short-term pain in the markets.
- *Sovereign wealth funds (SWFs)* invest funds on behalf of their nations. Many such funds, like those in the Middle East, are simply investing surplus government reserves; some may also cover public pension obligations in their countries. One estimate puts the worldwide total at $5.2 trillion. SWFs made headlines for large investments in banks weakened by the economic crisis, but some SWF investments are a little more glittery—witness the 5.2 percent stake in Tiffany owned by the sovereign wealth fund of Qatar.

Other types of institutions include investment banks and trusts, and some refer to hedge funds and private equity as institutions.

Why You Should Care

Institutions still make up the lion's share of stock, bond, and commodity investment in the markets. They weigh heavily on market performance and overall economic performance, and on the allocation of capital to public and private enterprises. Your fortunes in these markets will depend in part on what institutions are doing, and in some cases, like insurance investments, investment performance may affect your personal finances.

76. MONEY MARKET FUND

Money market funds (MMFs), or money market *mutual* funds, specialize in investing cash assets in short-term securities to provide investors with slightly higher returns than banks, and liquidity—that is, unrestricted deposits and withdrawals. As a place for investors to park short-term cash, which is then used by public and private enterprises to fund short-term operations, money market funds perform a vital role in the economy.

What You Should Know

Money market funds are technically mutual funds, regulated by the Investment Company Act of 1940 (see #43) and subject to price variations based on performance of underlying assets. However, because money market funds invest in very price-stable, short-term debt securities (usually a "weighted average maturity" of ninety days or less), the asset base is extremely stable. As a result, the price of most money market fund shares is $1, and it is highly unusual for such a fund to "break the buck." It did happen, however, to two funds in the 2008 crisis as a result of investments they had made in failed investment bank

Lehman Brothers. Reserve Primary Fund fell to ninety-seven cents and the other, BNY Mellon, fell to ninety-nine cents—so you can see how stable these holdings are.

Most money market funds pay yields based on short-term interest rates, which in 2013 were practically nothing, below 0.2 percent in most cases. In more normal interest rate environments, money market funds pay 0.5 percent to 1.5 percent more than comparable bank savings instruments.

Money market funds are different from the assortment of money market accounts (MMAs) offered by banks. The bank MMAs pay slightly less than MMFs, but are not for the most part covered by FDIC insurance (see #45 Federal Deposit Insurance Corporation). Most money market funds are sold by mutual fund companies or are available through brokers, retirement plan administrators, and others. Most money market funds are taxable—that is, the interest earned is taxable—but some are based on government securities (for stability) or tax-exempt securities (for tax preference). Most MMFs charge modest fees, but in today's low interest rate climate, even a tenth of a percent makes a big difference.

Why You Should Care

Money market funds are a good place to park reserve cash—reserved either to invest or to handle unexpected emergencies in your personal finances. They offer stability and liquidity, and did offer somewhat better yields in the past.

77. CREDIT RATING AGENCY

Credit rating agencies are specialized companies that evaluate the financial strength of other companies and of the debt instruments they issue. These ratings are used by banks, lenders, and others interested in corporate strength to judge the safety and quality of debt. While credit rating agencies are important to the proper function of the financial system, they might not have been mentioned in this book, except for the large role they played in the 2008–2009 financial crisis and the Great Recession that resulted.

What You Should Know

Credit rating agencies evaluate the overall strength of credit and credit risk of a company, similar to the so-called "credit rating" you might receive as a consumer, and they also evaluate the strength and quality of specific debt issues, like bonds or commercial paper. The "big three" ratings agencies evaluating U.S. companies are Standard & Poor's, Moody's, and Fitch Ratings. They each have their own set of rating criteria, and each issues ratings more or less analogous to school letter grades, although the exact grading scale used by all three is different. Companies will usually get a credit risk rating as a whole, and most large corporations are rated by all three agencies. Individual securities will also get ratings, but typically from only one agency. Special securities issued by companies, like asset-backed securities (see #67), also get ratings, and it was these ratings that brought credit rating agencies into the spotlight after the financial crisis.

Credit ratings are, in theory at least, convenient and independently calculated tools to help others make fast decisions about whether to lend to or invest in companies. For the most part they work, and have been the standard for years. But ratings agencies and their ratings came into question in the wake of the 2008–2009 crisis for two primary reasons. First, they tend not to change fast enough to reflect current economic or corporate conditions. Second, and perhaps more damaging, is the apparent conflict of interest in their creation: the firm issuing securities hires the rating agencies to provide the rating. Naturally, the agencies try to please their customer for the sake of future business and the business relationship. But those attempts to please have been called into question, particularly with the number of highly rated mortgage-backed securities that blew up in the crisis.

To be fair, it isn't just the conflict of interest at fault—most likely, these securities were just too complex, and backed by assets too difficult to value, for any such rating to be accurate. Legislative reform of the ratings agencies has been slow in coming, but since reputation is the chief asset these companies have to sell, there has been a fair amount of self-reform, and their public image and effectiveness has returned to a large extent since the crisis.

Why You Should Care

Agencies rate debt securities that ultimately may include loans or mortgages you take out, and the ability of a rating agency to rate them fairly will determine how easily they can be sold to investors, ultimately affecting your ability to get financing. So there's no direct impact on you or your household, but ratings agencies are part of the machinery that makes financing—money—available to you at an appropriate price.

78. STOCKS, STOCK MARKETS, AND STOCK EXCHANGES

As recently as 1960, only about 10 percent of all households owned shares of stock in corporations. Today, due in part to individual retirement savings needs, that figure has grown to exceed 50 percent; that is, one in two households across the United States own shares of corporations.

The discussion of stocks and stock markets cannot be possibly completed in this small of a space; it's the subject for an entire book. What's important to know is that *stock* represents the owners' interest in a corporation, that interest is divided into *shares*, and that those shares are traded on one or more *stock exchanges* that comprise the *stock market*.

What You Should Know

Stocks can be listed on stock exchanges if they meet certain criteria in terms of size, volume, and share price given by the exchange. The exchange is a corporation or organization set up to bring buyers and sellers together, either in person or electronically. The exchange handles all incoming orders, executes them by matching a buyer to a seller, and routes the proceeds as funds to the appropriate parties.

The two major U.S. stock exchanges continue to be household names: the New York Stock Exchange (NYSE EuroNext) and the NASDAQ, which originally stood for the National Association of Securities Dealers Automated Quotations. In addition, the over-the-counter (OTC) and Pink Sheets markets and a series of regional exchanges handle specialized trading situations in the United States, and a network of online-only electronic exchanges has emerged, such as BATS Global Markets and Direct Edge, which have recently announced plans to combine to become the second-largest exchange in the U.S. by trading volume, ahead of NASDAQ. Most countries also have at least one major stock exchange.

How stock trades are actually executed varies by exchange. The original approach begun in the early 1790s on the corner of Wall and Broad Streets in Lower Manhattan eventually became the mainstay of the NYSE. That approach uses a *specialist*—an individual with assistants who manually matches buy and sell orders with each other and with a personal inventory when such external orders don't exist or are too few. Each stock has one specialist and one only; that specialist is assigned the task of maintaining orderly markets.

The specialist system obviously predates computers; the advent of computers naturally brought new, faster, and more transparent technologies to stock trading practice. The first change came in 1971 with the advent of the NASDAQ. Prior to the NASDAQ, the only alternative to the specialist system was a network of securities dealers hooked to each other by telephone; these dealers traded the stock, mostly of small or emerging companies "over the counter." The NASDAQ created a virtual marketplace accessed by computers where buyers and sellers, mostly dealers, posted quotes and executed trades against those quotes. Dealers could trade with the big brokerage houses to fill end-customer orders, and the late 1990s advent of personal computer and networking technology enabled individual traders to also access these markets. The day-trading craze of the late 1990s was the end result, and such high-powered direct access trading still goes on today.

Gradually and not surprisingly the specialist system is quickly becoming outmoded and replaced by faster, cheaper, and more transparent electronic tools; even the NYSE has evolved to electronic trading for a significant share of its volume. The specialist system still survives mostly to handle larger institutional trades.

Why You Should Care
The stock market and its effective operation are vital to a capitalist society. It is how capital is allocated between individuals, their representatives, and the corporations that need that capital. Without a fair or efficient market, that allocation wouldn't work well, and people would be fearful of investing in companies.

79. BONDS AND BOND MARKETS

Bonds are securities bought and sold by investors promising repayment by a certain date (*maturity*) with a certain *yield*, or interest amount, paid usually semiannually. Not surprisingly, bonds and other debt securities are sold in the bond market.

What You Should Know

Trading in the bond market sets the price of the bond, which in turn sets the *effective yield* on the bond. Suppose a bond pays 7 percent at *par*—that is, at $100 in price, the typical original sale amount and ultimate value paid back at maturity. That means that the bond pays $70 per year in interest on a $1,000 bond (the normal trading increment). If the market thinks that bonds are worth less, and drives the price down to $95 ($950 face value), the effective yield rises to 7.37 percent—interest rates go up. Remember, when bond prices go down, interest rates go up, and vice versa.

Carrying the discussion one step further, even if the bond falls to $95 ($950), eventually $1,000 will be repaid to the bondholder. So the *yield to maturity* captures not just the interest paid, but also the additional $50 recovered at maturity. Suppose the 7 percent bond matures in ten years. The yield to maturity would be 7.72 percent—a fairly complex calculation best done on a financial calculator.

Most bonds are traded "over the counter" between individual securities dealers, rather than on a transparent, electronic-driven market like the NYSE or the NASDAQ. Today's bond market looks more like the stock market of the 1960s and 1970s. Bonds are traded this way because each is unique—different issuer, different interest rate, maturity, and other terms and conditions. And most bonds are held longer and traded less frequently than stocks. The bond markets are less consumer-friendly—in part because consumers participate less in the bond markets; it is more of an institutional investor playground (see #75 Institutional Investors).

There are four categories of bonds and bond markets—corporate, government and agency, municipal, and asset-backed securities (see #67). The U.S. Treasury sells a lot of bonds, and has made the purchase of Treasury bonds among the most friendly of bond markets for the average consumer with its bond purchase website *www.treasurydirect.gov*.

Why You Should Care

Aside from being a place to buy and sell bonds by matching supply and demand for bonds, the bond market effectively determines interest rates. A rising bond market means falling interest rates; a falling bond market signals that interest rates are on the rise. If you're in the market yourself to "sell a bond of your own"—that is, to get a mortgage or some other large loan—watching the bond markets to see the direction of interest rates can be especially helpful.

80. COMMODITIES, FUTURES, AND FUTURES MARKETS

Commodities are physical materials and assets used in production of goods and services (like oil or corn or platinum) or as a store of value (like gold) or both (like silver). Many businesses buy commodities in large quantities to support their production, while other businesses, like mining companies or farms or agricultural producers, sell commodities in large quantities; that's their business.

Commodity *futures* are derivatives (see #66), securities products designed to provide a convenient way to buy and sell commodities, while commodity *futures markets* provide a way for buyers and sellers to trade those commodity futures.

What You Should Know

Futures contracts are standardized contracts to buy or sell a specified item, usually but not always a commodity, in a standardized quantity on a specific date. Commodity futures include agricultural products, shown in some listings as grains; "softs," like cotton, sugar, and coffee; meats; and mineral and mining products like metals and energy products. Futures contracts also go beyond commodities into *financial* futures, which include interest rates, currencies (see #81 Currency Markets/FOREX), and stock index futures. In fact, many more exotic futures products are coming to market for things like the weather, pollution credits, and so forth.

Futures contracts are typically set up for larger quantities of a commodity than any individual consumer would normally need. For instance, the standard contract size for gasoline futures is 42,000 gallons, quite a bit more than you'll need, even if you own the largest SUV. At $3 a gallon or so, on paper this is a $126,000 investment that few individuals would be able to make. So doesn't this discourage participation in the market? Not really, because commodities traders can borrow on *margin* (see #86) to finance most of the purchase. In the case of gasoline futures, a $6,000 upfront cash payment gets you in. As you can see, the leverage is high—a 10 percent increase in the price of gas ($12,600 on the contract) would almost triple the initial investment. However, if the price goes down, your $6,000 disappears quickly; when gone, your position is liquidated. That affords some downside protection.

Futures contracts are bought and sold by producers and consumers of the commodities involved. Producers like farmers or energy companies are looking to *hedge*, or protect, against future price *decreases*, while consumers like manufacturing companies are hedging against price *increases*. But there aren't that many producing or consuming businesses in the market at any given time for, say, copper. The markets are made complete by speculators, short-term investors trying to make a profit by guessing the future direction of the price of a commodity. While many speculators rarely see the actual cotton, they do play an important role in the determination of the price of cotton.

In many cases, the underlying assets to a futures contract may not be traditional commodities at all. For financial futures, the underlying assets or items can be currencies, securities, or financial instruments and intangible assets or referenced items such as stock indexes and interest rates. The "future" is the future price of the instrument, not the physical commodity.

Futures are traded on special markets set up to trade them, the most important of which are the Chicago Board of Trade (CBOT), the Chicago Mercantile Exchange (CME), and the New York Mercantile Exchange (NYMEX).

Why You Should Care

Commodities markets serve the economy as an important way to set prices on key materials that the economy depends on, both now and in the future. Ultimately, the price of the coffee you drink or the gas you buy is determined by what happens in the commodities markets. Commodity futures also provide a way—albeit not the only way—to invest in the perceived future scarcity of materials like oil, and in the performance of the economy in general.

Commodity traders like to point out that there is less "headline risk" in commodities—that is, there's no CEO or CFO to be caught fudging the books, for instance. Many of the human factors that add risk to stocks, bonds, and other investments are not present in commodities; investors consider commodities to be more of a "pure" investment.

81. CURRENCY MARKETS/FOREX

The exchange of national currency is vital in the course of national trade, and thus in the course of international economics. We cannot buy Japanese cars (produced in Japan, anyway) without first buying Japanese yen, and the Japanese can't buy U.S. rice without first buying U.S. dollars. So that need to support trade has given rise to foreign currency exchange markets to allow market participants to exchange currency, and in many cases to set the price, or rate, of that currency exchange.

What You Should Know

The dynamics of currency exchange and exchange rates are complex and covered in more depth in Chapter 8. Here, we'll talk about the foreign exchange markets themselves (known as "FOREX" or simply "FX"), and how they work.

Like commodity futures (see #80 Commodities, Futures, and Futures Markets), foreign exchange is a bigger market and plays a greater role than simply as a place for buyers and sellers of foreign goods to acquire the needed currency. Banks, large businesses, central banks, and governments use the FOREX markets to hedge positions, and even to implement policy, buying or selling currencies to achieve an exchange rate objective. And also like commodities, a considerable number of speculators and short-term traders "bet" on moves in currencies with relation to each other, adding market volume and liquidity to make exchange rates truly reflect the supply and demand of the moment.

Foreign exchange markets have grown enormously with the increase in international trade and the tendency since the early 1970s for countries to let their currencies "float"—that is, trade freely with a market-determined exchange rate. The average *daily* volume of FOREX transactions in 2013 was about $3 *trillion*, up from $2 *trillion* at the end of 2011 and $761 *billion* in 2008—phenomenal numbers. More than half of that volume is represented by dollar-euro and dollar-yen trades, according to the Foreign Exchange Committee's Survey of North American Foreign Exchange Volume.

Foreign currencies can be traded outright as "spot" trades, or as futures, forwards, or swaps. FX markets are more like bond markets than stock markets—a loosely connected confederation of electronically connected, over-the-counter dealers, rather than a centralized market or exchange. By nature the markets work across borders, and thus aren't subject to much regulation from any single country. There really isn't any one single exchange rate; it is more a matter of the last trade that shows up "on the tape"— the electronic record from actual trades, and of the current dealer quotes being offered. Although these markets are set up more for large institutions and full-time players, most "retail" investors access these markets through specialized brokers set up for currency trading. Most retail investors play these markets through futures, which employ margin to expand the size of the transaction. More recently, regulators have moved toward allowing ordinary retail brokers to handle FX trading for their clients.

Why You Should Care

The exchange of currency is vital to the function of the growing global economy. While outright currency trading is complex and best left to specialists or dedicated individuals, the outcome of FOREX trading can have a big effect on what you pay for foreign goods, and on the greater health of the economy.

82. BROKERS, BROKER DEALERS, AND REGISTERED INVESTMENT ADVISERS

Your good friend John Smith, a registered investment adviser, wants your business. He wants to help you by investing your savings and managing those investments.

Your good friend Mary Jones, a broker working for You-NameIt Securities, a registered broker-dealer, also wants your business. She also wants to help you manage your investments.

What should you do? What do these people do, and what is their premise and promise in the management of your assets? Broker-dealers and registered investment advisers perform an important role in helping individuals (and corporations and institutions) manage their money, since perhaps they don't have the time, expertise, and interest in doing so. It's a service like any other service. But it's good to know a few things about what these folks do, how they're regulated, and what the pitfalls are before you pick one, if you decide that the "do it yourself" choice isn't an option.

What You Should Know

A broker-dealer is a company set up and in business to trade securities—stocks, bonds, and commodities—for its customers (as "broker") or on its own account (as "dealer"). Most broker-dealers participate in the markets to make money for their own benefit. A broker-dealer is a corporation or some other business form, not an individual. Many broker-dealers are actually subsidiaries of larger firms—banks or other financial services companies.

Broker-dealers are regulated under the Securities Exchange Act of 1934 by the SEC (see #43 and #44). They are also self-regulated to a degree through a familiar trade industry group known as the Financial Industry Regulatory Authority (FINRA), formerly known as the more familiar National Association of Securities Dealers (NASD).

Registered investment advisers (RIAs), on the other hand, can be individuals or firms registered with the SEC or a state regulatory body to manage the investments of others. RIAs can work independently, for RIA firms, for broker-dealers, or for other non-RIA firms.

An RIA must pass an exam (FINRA's Series 65 Uniform Registered Investment Adviser Law Exam) or show equivalent professional competence, fill out forms, and pay filing fees, but there is no required curriculum or technical standard of performance. The standards are more centered on customer care, including the commitment to act in a "fiduciary capacity" by always placing the interest of a client in front of personal interest. There are also standards for disclosure and avoiding conflicts of interest. These legal responsibilities are well known but can be difficult to enforce in practice; RIAs must keep accurate records and file periodic reports. RIAs are usually paid on a fee-for-service basis, while broker-dealers are typically compensated by per-transaction commissions.

The key difference between broker-dealers and RIAs in practice is liability: RIAs can be liable for the advice they give, while broker-dealers as firms are not. Further, there is no clear regulation of the conflict of interest in a broker dealing in the same securities for its own account while advising you to buy or sell them; it's a bit like doctors making money from the drugs they prescribe for you. Not that this conflict comes into play continually, but it happens, and it's something to be aware of.

Why You Should Care

Obviously, not all broker-dealers are bad, and not all RIAs are good. Read the disclosure documents and discuss them carefully to know who or what you're working with, and keep the fiduciary standard in mind as you observe your adviser's behavior and actions.

83. FINANCIAL ADVISERS

Let's suppose you need not only investment advice, but also advice on handling your overall finances. You need the right insurance. You need to plan for college and retirement. You need to figure out how much money you need now and in the future, and how to provide for yourself, your family, and the eventual financial legacy you leave to your loved ones.

Unless you're the strong, silent, do-it-yourself type (and there are a lot of you out there), you need a financial adviser.

What You Should Know

Financial advisers are paid professionals who learn your financial situation, develop financial plans for you and your family, and help you find the tools—investments, savings plans, insurance, legal advice—to execute the plan. A good financial adviser looks at your personal and family goals, translates them to short- and long-term financial needs, and then develops, documents, and reviews a complete plan to meet the goals and needs.

Depending on the adviser, some may implement all or part of the plan—if they are registered investment advisers (see #82 Brokers, Broker Dealers, and Registered Investment Advisers) too, they may buy and sell securities on your behalf. If they are licensed insurance salespeople, they can sell insurance. If they are CPAs, they can do your taxes. If they are attorneys, they can execute trusts and estate plans. You get the idea.

There are two primary types of financial advisers, distinguished by the way they are paid. *Fee-based* advisers typically charge a mix of flat fees and per-transaction fees. The flat fees are tied to your asset base for general services; the per-transaction fees may be collected from you or from the providers of the securities they sell as commissions. Some criticize fee-based advisers for having an inherent conflict of interest, making money for selling XYZ family of mutual funds while supposedly also acting in your interest. *Fee-only* advisers don't collect commissions, which reduces the risk of a conflict of interest between the adviser and the client if the adviser is beholden to another financial institution.

Financial advisers can come with a large assortment of credentials, some of which are more impressive than others. The Certified Financial Planner (CFP) is considered the highest in the food chain, with requirements for education, examination, and experience before practicing in the profession, and a strong fiduciary commitment to act in your interest besides. You'll also see credentials like CLU (Chartered Life Underwriter) that point to a specialty in insurance, but many of these credentials also cover other elements of the financial planning process. For more on financial advisers and the financial planning process, the Financial Planning Association (*www.fpanet.org*) is a good resource.

Why You Should Care

As with most services, you should shop carefully for a financial adviser. Checking references, getting examples of what they've done for others, and checking credentials, experience, attitude, and personality all can play a part. They work for you, and their purpose, as well as their best interest, is to serve *your* needs.

84. ELECTRONIC AND HIGH-FREQUENCY TRADING

Few industries have been revolutionized as much by technology as the trading of securities—stocks, bonds, futures, and the like. Electronic trading has speeded the function of the markets to the point where trades can be executed on a global basis almost instantaneously. That has in turn speeded up the pace of change and increased the need for quick decision making at all levels of business and government—and has spurred a whole new approach to securities trading, where algorithms and computer models can replace a considerable amount if not all human thinking and decision making. The effects are huge. We got a hint as we witnessed the 2008 market meltdown; there was scarcely any time to react as global markets swooned on even the slightest news. We got another big hint—really, a kick in the side of the head—during the so-called "flash crash" of May 2010, where computerized trading froze up due to a relatively simple set of triggering events, and the market plunged—for a few minutes. So while electronic trading only affects those traders in a given securities markets on the surface, the global impacts can be a lot larger.

What You Should Know

For most of history, stock and other securities markets were physical markets like the NYSE, where people actually met face-to-face and traded stocks and securities (see #78 Stocks, Stock Markets, and Stock Exchanges). Communications like telephones and teletype machines connected those humans with other humans at exchanges, at securities dealers around the country, and in a few cases, around the globe. Those communications were rapid, but were only point-to-point—that is, one sender to one receiver—and the entire process was only as fast as the interaction of the humans at the end of the communication chain.

Improvements in communications and technology, notably networked computers, made it less important for buyers and sellers to work face-to-face. The NASDAQ automated quote system allowed market participants—dealers—to come together by posting quotes electronically; the entire market was visible to market players with the right level of access. This advance greatly superseded point-to-point communications; the markets could handle the actions of many participants at once. Personal technology allowed individuals to work in markets once restricted to big trading firms with large computer installations. Beyond the actual execution of electronic markets, all market players also had real-time access to information, including quotes, news releases, and company information.

Today's trading is becoming more electronic, with buyers and sellers coming together on electronic quote boards known as electronic communications networks (ECNs). Some ECNs like Arca have been absorbed as part of the major exchanges (the NYSE in Arca's case), providing an electronic trading platform within the exchange. The rapidly growing (and combining) BATS, Direct Edge, and other electronic markets noted in

#78 have provided another major trading venue. Sophisticated "client" algorithms and triggers automate the entry of orders when certain price conditions have been met, and have enabled one computer to trade with another computer through the electronic network; humans barely need to be involved, except to set the conditions of order entry.

So-called "high-frequency trading," where orders are triggered by algorithms and executed in milliseconds, even nanoseconds, accounts for some 50 percent of all stock market volume. High-frequency traders are attempting to capture tiny gains, over and over, by getting information "first," and by capturing small differences in prices among markets, often less than a penny per share. High-frequency trading, while providing "liquidity"—volume and execution speed—to the markets, has also been described as unfair, as direct connects to exchange computers and newswire services give large firms involved in the game an unfair advantage. A recent ruling denied the release of University of Michigan's Index of Consumer Sentiment indicators to certain traders (who paid extra) *two seconds* before the broadcast release, on the grounds that it was "insider information" giving advantage to those traders (see #85 Insider Trading).

Why You Should Care

If you're a stock or other securities trader, it's important to understand how the different trading platforms and markets work. If you're not an active trader, it's still good to be familiar with the forces behind today's markets, and to be aware of how fast things can change, and why.

85. INSIDER TRADING

Suppose you wanted to buy into the corner ice cream store. It looks like a great investment, and the "fringe benefits" of being an owner seem appealing too. So the founder and majority owner offers to let you buy shares. You're happy about your investment, and ready to cash in (and eat) the proceeds. Everything goes well; your investment rises in value, and you get a nice discount on two-scoop helpings of chocolate peanut butter ice cream besides. Eventually you need the money for something else, and sell for a reasonable profit.

Shortly afterward, you find out that a major operator of ice cream parlors wants to add that store to its chain, and is willing to pay a handsome price for it. Then, in a casual conversation with your neighbor across the fence, you find out that she bought a boatload of stock at a ridiculously low price because the founder/owner gave her a tip that this might happen. She got a tip; you didn't. She bought; you sold. Is that fair? Should you, also an owner—and other owners—have been privy to the same news before you sold?

Although we're dealing with a small business, not a big, publicly traded corporation, you've been a victim of insider trading. An insider got information you weren't privy to, and made money on it. What happened here isn't technically illegal because the ice cream parlor wasn't "public," but it gives you an idea of what could happen when owners, directors, key managers, or employees disclose certain private information to privileged investors and not to everyone.

What You Should Know

Insider trading is the illegal trading of a public company's stock or other securities based on "insider information"—information acquired as, by, or from someone who creates or has access to privileged information about a company not available to the general public. "Insiders" include company officers, directors, or beneficial owners (more than 10 percent) of a company's stock. The general rule is that employees, by virtue of employment, put shareholder interests ahead of their own—all shareholders' interests—so disclosing inside information to certain shareholders violates this principle.

That said, especially in today's teleconnected world, you can see how easy it would be, say, for a large hedge fund manager or individual investor to get—or even buy—the "inside scoop" from even a fairly low-level employee and trade big on the tip. Think of what someone in a financial reporting, sales, or even a shipping department might know about a company's products and prospects. Think of what professional securities analysts, who make their living talking to companies and following their fortunes, might know, act on, and disseminate illegally before the general public finds out. Think of what politicians and government officials, who might know what contracts are coming up or what purchases are about to be made, could do.

Several high-profile insider-trading cases have come up in recent years, and recent rulings have strengthened the hand of regulators to go after the perpetrators. Former hedge fund manager Raj Rajaratnam was sentenced to eleven years for his role in an insider-trading ring, where he set up at least four different insiders, three of whom were Harvard classmates, to pass information his way. This high-profile case has led to a greater crackdown on the activity, but it remains difficult to enforce, and especially to gain convictions. Still, the prospects of greater enforcement and jail terms have sent a powerful signal to corporate executives about disclosing anything that might be considered sensitive information.

Why You Should Care

First, if you're an investor, know that you're putting a lot of pressure on your friends and colleagues if you ask them to tell you what's going on in the companies they work for. And if you work for a public company, be careful about what you tell others around you. Aside from that, insider trading has led to untold millions in profits for the perpetrators, at least indirectly at your expense. On the flip side, many feel that the recent crackdown has led to faster disclosure of information to the general public (once available to everyone, it isn't "insider" any more), a good thing for all investors.

86. MARGIN AND BUYING ON MARGIN

Buying on margin refers to borrowing from your broker to buy a security, usually a stock, a bond, or a futures contract. The security, or other securities in your portfolio, is used as collateral. When you borrow to buy on margin, you pay margin interest rates set by the broker, usually a fairly high rate, but not as high as a credit card. Margin buyers are trying to buy larger positions than they can afford out of pocket in order to get more exposure—leverage—from their investments.

What You Should Know

To buy on margin, you must set up a margin account with your broker. Typically that means depositing a certain amount and signing several forms indicating you understand the terms and conditions. This can be done online with online brokers. And not all securities are *marginable*; some low-price or risky stocks, for instance, do not qualify for margin buying.

When you buy a security on margin, you must have enough collateral to make the purchase. This test comes in the form of a *margin requirement*, 50 percent for stocks, set by the Federal Reserve in the wake of the 1929 stock market crash. That means you must have at least 50 percent of the entire purchase available in your account as cash or equity. This is, of course, to prohibit you from borrowing too much, as many did in 1929 and before, when they borrowed up to 90 percent of their securities purchases.

That 50 percent requirement only applies to the initial purchase. After that, rules set by your broker apply. There is a *minimum maintenance requirement* below which your equity portion will trigger a sale or a request for more equity (cash) to be whole—this is a *margin call*. A typical minimum maintenance requirement is 35 percent, meaning that once your equity falls below 35 percent of the entire stock position, you get the call. So if you buy 100 shares of a $10 stock for $1,000, you can borrow $500 of the $1,000. If the stock drops below the point where the equity portion of the investment is 35 percent, you'll trigger the call.

What is that price? The formula is: Borrowed Amount/(1–Maintenance Requirement). Got that? So if the maintenance requirement is 0.35 and you borrowed $500, the formula would give you the total securities value to match 35 percent, in this case $500/(0.65), or $769.23. That means that if your $10 stock goes down to $7.69, you will get a margin call.

Margin positions are evaluated each night for sufficient equity. The calculation of margin sufficiency is more complex with multiple securities in an account. Also, this example applies to stocks; the initial and maintenance margin requirements are different for commodities.

Why You Should Care

Margin can add power to your investment portfolio, but like any other borrowing, it can be dangerous, and should be treated accordingly. Margin interest rates, while moderately high, can be lower than some other forms of short-term borrowing, so it might make sense to use margin to get some cash from your investment account for certain purposes. On a larger scale, when stock margin borrowing levels increase in aggregate, it's a sign that too many people are speculating on stocks and that a bubble might be forming, leading to a bust later on.

87. SHORT SELLING

Short selling in financial markets is the practice of borrowing a security, usually a stock, and selling it in the market. The idea is to borrow and sell with the hopes of buying the security back, or *covering*, later at a lower price. It is done when you think the price of the security is too high. Note that short selling means something different in real estate (see #90 Foreclosure/Short Sale).

Short selling made the front pages during the height of the 2008–2009 market meltdown, when large hedge funds and short sellers drove down the prices of certain stocks, mostly in the financial sector. It was felt that short sellers "ganged up" on some of these stocks, creating an unnatural downward momentum. During that time the SEC initiated some short selling curbs on certain financial stocks, but many feel that such artificial curbs don't have much real effect on the markets—a "sick" stock will go down anyway, with or without the curbs.

What You Should Know

In stock market parlance, "going long" means you are buying the security; by "going short" you effectively own a negative quantity of a security. You owe the security and will pay margin rates (see #86) to borrow it, with many of the same margin rules in effect. In normal practice, you borrow the security from a real lender, arranged behind the scenes through the broker network. The lender is entitled to receive any dividends that may accrue during the borrowing period, and of course, to receive the shares back once the short sale is covered.

Short selling is inherently risky. Why? Because a stock can only go to zero on the downside, but rise, theoretically, to infinity on the upside. If it rises "to infinity and beyond," you're liable for the entire amount of that rise from the price you shorted it at.

Most short sellers are knowledgeable and seasoned professionals who employ good risk-management techniques to control potential large losses. In recent years there has been a rash of "naked" shorting, where sellers sell shares they don't borrow or have (sometimes such shares can be in short supply). Naked shorting probably exaggerated the slide during the financial crisis.

If a stock or other security is being sold short, that isn't always a bad thing for investors in that stock. Active short selling does mean that some investors—probably pretty good ones—are betting against the stock. It also adds supply to the market, driving prices down. But all shares sold short must be bought back, or covered, eventually, so assuming your company isn't going bankrupt, that demand will all come back to market sooner or later.

Why You Should Care

Short selling serves a useful purpose in allowing individual investors to bet against a stock or company. It also adds liquidity to the market, and prevents the market from rising beyond reality—it is sort of a check and balance on the markets.

Unless you're a fairly active and knowledgeable investor, short selling probably won't be in your bag of tricks. If you do sell short, you must choose wisely and be prepared to follow closely. When short selling becomes rampant in a market (not always easy to tell, for so-called short interest statistics are published only monthly), it's a sign of a "bear," or down, market. The reversal of a short selling pattern can be quite sharp to the upside, as short sellers rush to cover; this phenomenon is called a *short squeeze*. In sum, short selling isn't for the faint of heart; neither is owning stocks that are short seller favorites.

88. MEDIAN HOME PRICE

If you've been reading along, we've covered about every financial and financial market topic *except* real estate. For this and the next three tips, real estate assumes center stage.

Real estate is both a commodity and an investment. As a commodity it serves a useful purpose, and its price reflects the laws of supply and demand. As an investment, it requires an upfront purchase to generate cash returns later, either as income or as a capital gain upon selling the property. If you own your own home, those "cash returns" come in the form of rent you *don't* have to pay.

Real estate markets operate quite differently from other financial markets. As the saying goes, "all real estate markets are local." Aside from real estate investment trusts (REITs) and other investment vehicles, each piece of property is unique, and its price is determined by the supply and demand *in that local market*, as those of you who have tried to buy beachfront property or a home in the most expensive neighborhood in town already know.

Still, like all markets, we need some kind of pricing benchmark—like a market index, a commodity futures price, or an exchange rate—to know where that market stands compared to its past, and to determine how affordable a certain property is. That's where *median home price* enters the picture.

What You Should Know

Median home price is a statistics-based figure used to measure pricing in a given area. That area can be nationwide, regional, by state, by city, or even by neighborhood. For that geographic segment, the median home price means that half of the homes in a given area sold for more than the median price, and half of them sold for less.

If the national median price for single-family homes was $199,000 in mid-2013, that means that half of all of the single-family homes sold for more than $199,000 (think of those fancy mansions on the beach in Malibu), and half of them sold for less than $199,000 (think of the large numbers of modest homes in, say, St. Louis). That figure was over $230,000 in 2005 but dropped to $169,000 in 2009, so you can see how much the real estate market has fluctuated in recent years—and in many markets like Las Vegas and Phoenix it has fluctuated quite a bit more than that.

Median home prices are calculated by several agencies, the most prominent of which is the National Association of Realtors (NAR). The NAR publishes a quarterly list of Median Sales Price of Existing Single-Family Homes for Metropolitan Areas, with data stretching back to 1979. See *www.realtor.org/topics/*

metropolitan-median-area-prices-and-affordability/data and other resources on that site.

Why You Should Care

Median home prices affect you as a homebuyer on a few levels. Of course, it is a quick read on the real estate market, and whether your home is worth more or less than it was, say, this time last year. Since medians are just that—medians—it's important to look at median prices in your city, and better yet, in your neighborhood, to get an idea of your home's worth.

You might also consider the varying regional median prices as a litmus test for where you can actually afford to live. While the national average as of mid-2013 is $199,000, you can look at prices, and the inventory and sales figures, which affect prices, in your city at the National Association of Realtors databank mentioned above. You can get median prices at your neighborhood level on Zillow (*www.zillow.com*).

89. HOUSING AFFORDABILITY

Can you, or anyone else, afford a home in your area or in another area you might be hoping to live in? Clearly that's not an easy thing to figure out. Equally clearly, your ability to afford a home in a certain area is a function of your income, and the average incomes of those in that area. So to determine affordability, economists and real estate professionals take the median home price for any given area and compare it to the median income for the same area to determine whether or not the housing stock is actually affordable. Can the people who live and work there actually afford to buy what's on the market?

What You Should Know

The measurement of home prices was covered in the previous entry. But these home prices don't exist in a bubble; they exist in real communities that have real people with real jobs and incomes, and affordability actually lies in whether the average Joe in any given place can afford to buy at the median home price. If the median price for an existing single-family home in the West is at present $247,800, how many of the folks in that area make enough money to be able to comfortably afford that price?

In addition to median home prices, the NAR publishes the Housing Affordability Index. This index takes into account several factors, and gives you an idea of what it takes to afford a house in any given region.

The index, which is calculated over time and by region and is available at *www.realtor.org/topics/metropolitan-median-area-prices-and-affordability/data* under "Affordability Data," compares median home prices to median income and determines whether the median income affords *exactly* the median home (index=100), affords *more than* the median home (>100), or affords *less than* the median home (<100). Factors included in the affordability calculation include the median price, the average mortgage rate, monthly principal and interest payment (P&I), payment as a percentage of income, the median family income, and the qualifying income. The calculation assumes a down payment of 20 percent and a total P&I payment not exceeding 25 percent of median income.

Here's how the calculations work. Suppose we want a snapshot of housing affordability in the Midwest for example. Assuming a standard 20 percent down payment on a single-family house with the current median price of $143,100 at a mortgage rate of 3.66 percent and a thirty-year, fixed-rate mortgage (360 payments), the monthly P&I would be $526. This would be 10.1 percent of the $62,359 median family income in that area. In order to qualify for that loan you would have to have an income of $29,088, giving an affordability index of 206. So, is Midwest housing affordable based on this measure? You bet.

Why You Should Care

Housing affordability, like the median home prices, can help you determine whether a certain area or region can provide the kind of lifestyle you want at a reasonable price. Of course, beyond median family incomes, whether you can afford an area depends on what *you* earn, not the averages, and it depends on the home you choose. Still, housing affordability helps you make important lifestyle choices, and it also helps indicate whether real estate prices in a locale are in line with reality.

90. FORECLOSURE/SHORT SALE

Not too long ago, the words "appreciation" and "opportunity" were the first to come to mind when the topic of real estate came up. Then came the bubble and the bust, and the words "foreclosure" and "short sale" dominated the listings and the conversation. Since then, the number of foreclosures has dropped significantly, but they still stubbornly remain an important part of the market, at least for the time being.

Foreclosure is a formal process that occurs when an owner cannot pay the mortgage on a property, and ultimately transfers title on the property from the borrower to the lender. A short sale is designed to "short circuit" that process; it's an arranged distress sale to avoid the foreclosure. Both processes serve to get distressed owners out of an untenable situation, typically with both the lender and the borrower losing some in the deal.

What You Should Know

Foreclosure is a lengthy and costly process that typically starts with a *notice of default*, which goes out when a payment is 60–90 days overdue. At that point, as an owner/borrower, you still have time to cover the obligation or arrange an alternative. After 90–120 days, the notice of default turns into a *notice of sale* where a court determines that a lender can start sale proceedings and evict the owner. When the title is transferred to the lender, it is known as real estate owned (REO), especially if the lender is a bank. Banks and other lenders, as a result of the huge numbers of foreclosures that occurred in 2008–2010, ended up owning far more property than they knew what to do with (see #88 Median Home Price). Just as bad, the foreclosure process is estimated to cost the lender some $50,000 to $60,000 to carry out.

Because of the glut of REO and the cost of fully pursuing foreclosure, many lenders opted to accept proposed short sales. A short sale is a negotiated deal between the borrower/owner and lender to accept a lower price on a sale to a third party, and in turn the lender is willing to accept less than the full amount owed for a property on which they hold the mortgage. Often the seller has little or no equity and might even owe more than the property is currently worth, and the seller usually must convince the lender that the situation is due to financial hardship. Regardless, it can be a win-win, for the borrower/owner gets out of the home and doesn't take the hit of a foreclosure on the credit record, while the lender doesn't take on any more REO, saves fees, and doesn't have to worry about property deterioration while held as REO.

A borrower/owner must approach the lender for the short sale; the lender will not propose it. The owner must also show effort in trying to sell the property for market price for some period of time.

Why You Should Care

You don't want to go through foreclosure, if at all possible. Not only do you lose your home and any equity you might have built up in it, but your credit rating can be blemished for as long as ten years. If you're in trouble, you should evaluate all options, including short sales, deed in lieu of foreclosure (where you simply hand the keys back to the bank), and an assortment of government programs that continue to be in force, although they tend to have fairly strict qualification guidelines.

It's also worth learning the mechanics of foreclosure if you're a buyer. Foreclosures and short sales signal opportunity, and if you play the game right, you can still get a bargain. Most local realtors have developed the skills and knowledge (by necessity!) to deal in foreclosed homes.

CHAPTER 8

Trade and International Economics

Even on our small planet, no nation exists in a vacuum. Sure, the United States is blessed with abundant resources to grow food, build shelter, and accomplish the routine tasks of daily life. But we don't have everything. We've always been dependent on foreign nations for some things like coffee or saffron spice or chromium. We had become increasingly dependent on other nations for energy, but with recent domestic production through so-called "fracking," that's become less true, demonstrating once again that necessity is the mother of invention. But that said, increasingly, we've found that many of the goods and services we need can be produced elsewhere for less—although that trend, too, is showing some signs of reversing. In general, global trade has its advantages and disadvantages, which will be further explored in this chapter in the discussion of *globalization*.

At the same time, foreign societies need American goods and services. In general, all countries need things that other countries produce, giving rise to a global economy consisting of many local economies and a trade system to connect them. Foreign trade has existed since the days of Marco Polo (and before), but as technology and economic development make the world more interconnected and "flatter," foreign trade assumes an increasingly important role in our own personal "economy." We buy things made overseas. We produce things that we hope will sell overseas. Overseas competition forces us to be more efficient, and when we can no longer compete, we must find something else to do. Globalization and its effects have touched millions of us, and it is often a difficult pill to swallow.

While globalization can cause pain, it's here, it's with us, and it also has important benefits to our economy. As individuals, we need to turn fear into an understanding of the forces of globalization, as well as the rules and tools of international trade. That's the subject of this final chapter.

91. GLOBALIZATION

You can buy cars made in Asia. You can buy cars made by Asian companies in America or American companies in Mexico or—you name it. You can buy a computer, smartphone, or tablet manufactured by an American company in Asia, or by a Chinese company in China or in Vietnam or wherever, and if you need help using it, you call someone in India. For that matter, if you have a question about your employee benefits, such as how your U.S.-based 401(k) plan works, you might also end up talking to someone in India.

What's going on here? Simply, it's the inevitable march of *globalization*, the ever-increasing network of economic activity around the world.

What You Should Know

Globalization happens because it *can* happen; that is, the technologies exist to interconnect different economies and their productive components cheaply and easily. Your benefits phone call to India simply wouldn't work without current phone and data technologies, and it wouldn't work if it cost a dollar a minute to make the call. It is also made possible by *free trade*, where few artificial barriers are put into play by governments to keep an economic activity within their borders.

Globalization is driven by economic specialization and so-called *comparative advantage*. Comparative advantage is simply the idea that some economies or some productive elements within an economy can do something better, cheaper, or faster than someone else. Highly skilled labor with English-language and technology skills is available in India at a low cost. China has an enormous pool of skilled and unskilled manufacturing labor. Japan has precision engineering and manufacturing, and Taiwan has heavy industrial manufacturing like foundries and semiconductor manufacturing facilities. These companies don't have a monopoly on these activities by any means, but they do them better than everyone else. They are leaders in the fields.

Globalization simply takes advantage of whoever can do whatever best. The natural forces of economics steer skilled software engineering and technical support to India, low-cost manufacturing to China, and precision instrument manufacturing to Germany or Japan. The networks are growing more complex, as Japanese companies now "reglobalize" some of their manufacturing to places like Thailand. It's a naturally evolving world order, which is estimated to save us all trillions over a closed-economy scenario where trade and technology are restricted within a country's borders.

Not everyone is behind the idea of globalization. It has obviously caused some of the painful job dislocations that have hurt American manufacturing. Many question whether saving a few pennies on a manufactured item is worth the loss of jobs and manufacturing infrastructure in the United States. Many also blame the exploitation of disadvantaged workers and physical environments, which can go so far as to even compromise their very safety, around the world on globalization. Finally, some take on globalization as a threat to unique world culture, just as the nationalization of business and marketing has voided U.S. regions of their local cultural imprint and made every freeway interchange across the country look like every other.

Globalization means change, and change can be painful. But the true benefits in terms of economic progress (yes, it helps poor economies too) and economic efficiencies cannot be ignored.

Why You Should Care

The news headlines and the stories you hear frequently center on the less positive effects of globalization—your neighbor gets laid off, a nearby factory closes. It probably doesn't make the pain go away for those affected, but if you put it in the greater context of globalization and economic efficiency, and realize that comparative advantage is the most important economic driver, you can put it in perspective. You as an individual, and your employer as a company, must strive to maintain that competitive advantage in a free-market economy, else globalization becomes a risk, not an opportunity.

92. CURRENCY POLICY AND EXCHANGE RATES

"The dollar declined today against the euro and gained against the yen but held its ground at $1.04 against the Canadian dollar."

Nice headline, but what does it mean? Sure, now my imaginary trip to Europe is a little more expensive, and it might help reduce the cost of my next new Lexus. But what's really going on here? How—and why—do currencies fluctuate against one another?

What You Should Know

Currency fluctuations, like most things that happen in free markets, are driven by supply and demand. If the euro is up against the dollar, it reflects the fact that world currency traders feel the euro is worth more and the dollar is worth less, and so buy euros and sell dollars. The important question is: why do they feel that way?

Purchases and sales of a currency are determined by actual monetary needs at a given point of time, which are in turn driven by physical and financial trade. *Physical trade* refers to who is buying and selling goods and services of each country. If more people are buying European or Japanese goods or services at a given point in time, they need currency in those countries to complete the purchase, and so buy it on the open market. They may also be *preparing* to buy such currency by buying a futures contract. Financial trade refers to the transfer of capital to buy securities or other investments in a country, which also requires a purchase of local currency. So if euro-denominated bonds look attractive due to credit risk or higher interest rates or price stability or some combination of the three, investors will buy euros in order to buy those bonds. It's not hard to see how these flows relate to balance of trade (see #95) and balance of payments (see #96).

Exchange rates don't just fluctuate based on *current* supply and demand for a currency, but also expected *future* supply and demand. If a country's economic indicators (or economic policies) signal declining production, higher deficits, more "printed" money, higher inflation, or declining interest rates ahead, currency traders will sell that country's currency in anticipation of those events. Political and economic stability can also come into play. These sentiments can drive markets in one direction or another for a considerable period of time even though actual economic statistics and trade flows ultimately fail to support the sentiment.

Not every currency "floats" against every other; for various political reasons, some countries choose to intervene or even tightly control their foreign exchange rates. When a currency is allowed to "float," free markets determine the exchange rates as just described, and the U.S., Japanese, Eurozone, and most other major European currencies do just that. "Floating" currency exchange rates are the "pure market."

A country may also decide to "fix" its currency against another, often but not always the U.S. dollar. The goal is price stability in the country and stabilization of foreign trade, and it is accomplished either by direct control or intervention in the open currency markets to keep the exchange rate stable. China is the biggest and most influential user of the fixed exchange rate approach. Many U.S. policymakers and industrialists criticize this approach for they feel that the Chinese renminbi (their exchangeable currency) is too low against the U.S. dollar, which serves to stimulate their exports at the expense of making it hard for U.S. firms to compete.

Why You Should Care

Even if you don't plan a trip to Europe or to buy a Japanese-manufactured automobile in the future, currency fluctuations can affect you, especially in the long term. The proliferation of U.S.-based factories for Japanese cars is driven (pardon the pun) by the long-term decline of the dollar against the yen. The abundance of cheap Chinese manufactured goods, supported by the Chinese government exchange rate "fix," helps tame U.S. inflation, but perhaps at the expense of long-term U.S. economic strength. Currency rates can be both a result of and a cause of economic change, and you should keep your finger on the pulse of such change.

93. CURRENCY DEVALUATION AND DEPRECIATION

When thinking in an economic frame of mind, the term "devaluation" suggests bad things—less value, less worth, less productivity, less to be had or shared by all. The term "depreciation" also suggests long-term, inexorable decay. These two words, in fact, describe deliberate economic policy a nation might employ to reduce the exchange rate of its currency on the world market. While often indicating heavy medicine for a very sick economic patient, such actions aren't always as bad as they sound.

What You Should Know

In the previous entry the role of currency exchange in the long-term economic prospects of a nation—and vice versa—were described. The distinction between floating and fixed, or controlled, exchange rates was also examined. Some countries take a more active role than others in controlling their exchange rates for clear political and economic reasons—to stimulate exports, to stimulate capital investments in their countries, and to achieve price stability within the country.

When a country fixes or closely manages its exchange rate, a central monetary authority (like a central bank) can decide to formally adopt a new fixed rate with respect to a foreign currency, usually but not always the U.S. dollar. That rate can be set by mandate or more often by government intervention in the currency markets. When a country chooses to lower its currency against the reference currency, that is known as *devaluation*. When a country chooses to intervene in the markets or adopt other policies that lead to a lower exchange rate, that's *depreciation*.

Devaluation is overt and is carried out publicly with fixed rate control; depreciation is carried out without specific declaration or obvious action. Both actions serve to make a currency, and thus the economy behind it, more attractive on the world stage, either for foreign purchases of goods and services or for foreign capital inflows or both.

Done right, a devaluation can help an economy, but done wrong or without warning, it can be quite disruptive. Currency devaluation caused an economic crisis in Mexico in 1994. The government decided to devalue to stem the tide of imports and keep a healthy trade balance, but did it suddenly and without warning. Those who had made investments in Mexico suddenly panicked over the value of their investments, withdrew capital, and sent the economy into a short tailspin. Untimely interventions also helped cause the Asian currency crisis in 1998.

Many economists are concerned by the U.S. Federal Reserve's apparent attempt to depreciate the dollar against other currencies. This is being accomplished by lowering interest rates and printing money in the interest of economic stimulus, and many regard it as a last-ditch effort to restore a healthy trade balance for American goods and services. But it could backfire if inflation takes root and causes America to lose its "safe haven" status for foreign investment. Similarly, and more recently, Japanese policies to reduce the value of the yen to stimulate trade and the internal economy have been met with skepticism—will they really work (especially in a "currency wars" environment where other major economies are depreciating their currencies too), and will it lead to excessive inflation later? Economists and world leaders thus watch any moves toward devaluation or depreciation very carefully.

Why You Should Care

Devaluation and the more covert depreciation can be used as short-term tools to stimulate an economy and balance it properly on the world stage. But they can also be used to stimulate an economy for short-term political gain. Such actions can be disruptive in the short term, and more importantly, can signal longer-term economic woes and unintended consequences to come. The economic forces and realities that caused these actions are often more important than the actions themselves.

94. FOREIGN DIRECT INVESTMENT

What do Pebble Beach Golf Links, Rockefeller Center, and the new Honda assembly plant in Greensburg, Indiana, have in common? They are owned, or have been owned, by foreign companies. When foreigners own U.S. property or business interests, it is known as foreign direct investment (FDI). It is the flip side of U.S. individuals or businesses owning foreign assets.

The amount of—and flow of—such investment holdings can be important indicators of economic health and prosperity.

What You Should Know

Foreigners can and do buy investment interest in U.S. businesses and properties. Technically, it happens when a foreign enterprise, or its affiliate, buys at least a 10 percent interest in a U.S. corporation or asset. Foreign direct investments do not include purchases of U.S. government securities or other similar investments—another huge inflow of investment funds.

The amount and balance of FDI has changed dramatically over the years. The relatively weak U.S. dollar and the continued status of the United States as a "safe haven" against world politics and economic events have caused a steady growth in FDI. The proximity of U.S. production resources to markets, as exemplified by automotive assembly, is another factor.

According to the U.S. Bureau of Economic Analysis, FDI flows into the United States ranged from $231 million to $58 billion annually during the years 1960–1995. These flows moved sharply upward to reach $321 billion in 2000, declined to $63 billion in 2003, ramped into the mid-$200 billions in 2006–07, and peaked at $325 billion in 2008. Then they dropped to $194 billion in 2010 and $146 billion in 2012 due to global economic conditions, low rates of return on U.S. investments, and the stronger dollar.

This sounds bad, and it's easy to think that Americans are selling themselves to foreigners one floor or golf hole at a time to pay off our debts. But the reality is a bit different; in fact, during much of this period, U.S. FDI in other nations was at similar or even higher levels. As a result, the growth in cross-border direct investment signals greater *globalization* (see #91), and indirectly, shifts of capital flows to the locations of greatest return.

Why You Should Care

Rather than taking umbrage when you find out that the Japanese or Chinese own your favorite golf course or restaurant or car company, consider cross-border investments to be natural. After all, we own those Starbucks outlets in China and Europe, right? The need for foreigners to finance U.S. debt is the bigger problem.

95. BALANCE OF TRADE

The balance of trade, much like the balance of your own household budget, measures the difference between goods and services purchased *from* foreigners and the goods and services purchased *by* foreigners from the United States. More concisely, the balance of trade is what we export minus what we import.

What You Should Know

The trade balance, or trade deficit, has been in the news a lot during the past thirty years, mainly because it has grown substantially as we buy more goods from overseas (especially China), more raw materials (oil from the Middle East and other nations), and other goods. On the services side, as we'll see in a minute, the United States runs a net surplus.

The balance of trade is part of a bigger picture known as the *current account*, or *balance of payments*. Those figures, covered in the next entry, include not only the trade balance in physical goods and services but investments and other financial flows. When there is a trade deficit, it is often made up by financial flows—that is, how we pay our bills, although under current practice it leaves us in debt.

The trade deficit has grown substantially since 1997. Before that time, it ranged between $50 billion and $100 billion each year. It grew to almost $400 billion in 2000 and then to nearly $800 billion in 2006, as the prosperous American economy led to more imports of finished goods and raw materials. The Great Recession, combined with lower oil prices, an increase in domestic oil production, and expanding "export" of services, have all combined to attenuate the total trade deficit somewhat. The following table shows how the deficit has fluctuated over time:

Table 8.1 U.S. Balance of Trade 2000–2012 ($ Billion)

Year	Total	Goods	Services
2000	−379,835	−454,690	74,855
2001	−365,505	−429,898	64,393
2002	−421,601	−482,831	61,230
2003	−495,035	−549,012	53,977
2004	−609,987	−671,835	61,848
2005	−715,269	−790,851	75,582
2006	−760,359	−847,260	86,901
2007	−701,423	−830,992	129,569
2008	−702,302	−833,957	131,655
2009	−383,657	−510,550	128,893
2010	−499,379	−650,156	150,777
2011	−556,359	−744,139	187,301
2012	−534,656	−741,475	208,819

Source: U.S. Census Bureau

Long term, the balance of trade is affected by the strength of the U.S. and global economy. While a strong global economy would seem to help reduce the deficit by increasing exports, in practice it has tended to increase the deficit as Americans import more. That trend may change as America becomes more energy self-sufficient, but as you can see in Figure 8.1, the recovery has brought a return to higher deficits again—though not as high as prior to the Great Recession.

Figure 8.1 Balance of Trade, 1992–2012

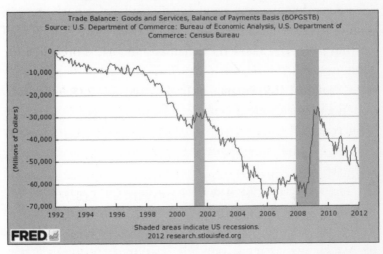

Source: St. Louis Federal Reserve

Whether the U.S. trade deficit is good, bad, or ugly is still a matter of debate. The good news is that deficits have bounced off their lows, and imports in particular, led by energy, appear to be headed for a long-term decline. Even more good news is found in the fact that the deficit as compared to the size of the economy is still relatively modest by world standards. And every dollar spent overseas at least has the potential to come back to shore as something bought from the United States.

But today's deficits are also a cause for major concern among economists and policymakers. First, they could well set new records again when the economy returns to health. Second, the gradual export of manufacturing capability to China and other nations suggests that the deficits may be structural and permanent and only likely to grow—although this trend has slowed lately. We just don't have enough to sell into world markets. Third, our trading partners, again notably China, must finance the deficit through investments in U.S. securities, which only pushes the problem into the future.

Governments, notably the U.S. government, may want to reduce deficits, but attempts to control deficits through policy, tariffs, or taxation are notoriously difficult and usually have negative unintended consequences elsewhere in the economy (see #98 Protectionism). In fact, government policy to stimulate consumption (see #2) has the opposite effect. When the government sent tax stimulus checks in 2008, or reduced FICA taxes in 2011–2012, how much of that money do you suppose was spent to buy foreign cars or electronic gadgets?

When governments stimulate consumption, especially here in the United States, they inadvertently stimulate the deficit too. Countries that have lower consumption patterns (indicated by higher savings rates) typically have trade surpluses (again, China, but also Germany, Japan, and others). One of the best ways to lower the deficit is to stimulate savings—although this too can get out of hand and lead to deflation (see #19), as has been the case in Japan.

Why You Should Care

Just as you need to keep your own financial house in order, you should also be concerned about a nation that consumes more from abroad than it produces. It's not a good thing over the long term. Not that you should or even can buy all of your goods from the United States, but all else being equal, a good or service sourced from the United States helps the economy, and one sourced from overseas hurts it.

96. BALANCE OF PAYMENTS AND CURRENT ACCOUNT

The balance of trade (covered in the previous entry) is part of a bigger trade picture. The balance of trade measures the flows of physical goods and services, and is a major component of the balance of payments. But the balance of payments goes further to measure the flow of payments—the financial flows—between countries. Thus, the flow of financial capital to purchase securities or to make foreign direct investments (see #94) is also included. It is a measure, at day's end, of how much total worth or wealth is coming out of or going into our collective wallet.

What You Should Know

You'll hear the term *current account* used frequently to determine where we are and where we are going. The current account is the sum of current activity from trade (imports and exports) and short-term financial flows like dividends and interest. The capital account—showing flows in favor of fixed asset investments and foreign direct investments—goes together with the current account to create the total balance of payments. Current account figures represent where we are short term with respect to international cash flows, and the current account deficit, like the trade deficit, gets a lot of attention from economists and policymakers.

Why You Should Care

Economists watch the balance of payments and the current account deficit or surplus to get the big picture on the health of the economy and the transfer of wealth from one nation to another. While knowing about the balance of payments may help you understand the evening news, it's the balance of trade that's truly important. As an individual, you can only affect the balance of trade through your consumption and saving decisions.

97. TRADE AGREEMENTS

Trade agreements, or trade "pacts," are made between countries, usually multiple countries in a region, to remove trade barriers and to facilitate trade between them. The goals are to encourage trade, to achieve gains from comparative advantage, and to mutually benefit the economies of the pact members. Trade agreements achieve the same results as globalization (see #91), but usually on a smaller, more regional scale.

What You Should Know

A trade pact is a negotiated agreement between countries stipulating terms of import and export of some or all goods and services that might flow between them. Agreements usually cover tariffs and other taxes, and in some cases may contain social, environmental, or other stipulations governing trade in mutually beneficial ways. Most are "free" trade agreements, allowing free movement of goods and services across member borders. Critics of trade agreements follow the path of globalization critics, and typically work to include environmental, labor, and product safety requirements in the agreements.

For Americans, the largest and most significant trade agreement in recent years is the North American Free Trade Agreement (NAFTA). The agreement, ratified in 1994 between the United States, Canada, and Mexico, is the largest in the world measured by combined purchasing power. NAFTA opened borders for almost unrestricted movement of goods and services, subject to environmental rules consistent with U.S. policy. NAFTA led to the opening of large *maquiladora* (border zone) factories in Mexico to serve Mexican markets, boosting Mexican economic growth to a degree.

Aside from a few industries like textiles and auto assembly, NAFTA didn't create the "giant sucking sound" famously promised by then-presidential candidate Ross Perot. According to a World Bank study (see #99), NAFTA did as much to strengthen exports out of the entire bloc as it did to increase American imports from Mexico. At the risk of gross oversimplification, NAFTA is a classic microcosm of globalization, where the comparative advantages of Mexico (abundant semiskilled labor), America (know-how), and Canada (resources) are combined to produce efficiencies and a more competitive larger player on the world stage.

NAFTA and its Central American sister CAFTA roll right off the tongue, but they are by no means our only major agreements. The United States has free trade agreements with twenty other countries, and is party to many bilateral and multilateral agreements. There are more than thirty operating trade agreements worldwide covering major regions of the world: Southeast Asia (ASEAN), the Middle East (GAFTA), and South America (Mercosur) serving as examples.

Why You Should Care

Trade agreements between countries or regions create economic efficiencies that usually result in lower prices for goods and services, and open new markets for businesses already located in member countries. These are both good things for you—so long as you aren't in a job or profession vulnerable to dislocation to one of the trading partners. In a larger sense, a rising tide of more competitive production lifts all boats, for the economies involved become more productive and more competitive on the world stage.

When one starts to see Mexican-made bars of soap on American store shelves, it could be time to step back—why can't that soap, a simple product, be made in America? Is the manufacturing cost so much lower that it overcomes transportation and all the administrative costs of moving it two thousand miles across a border? When economic dislocations become excessive one must examine the reasons why. Is Mexican labor cheaper or better, or is it simply that the cost of doing business in the United States—driven in part by health care costs—is too high? Free trade agreements can mask real problems in member economies—or make them worse than need be. As an individual, you should take advantage of less expensive goods and expanded markets but also be aware of the reasons driving the trade agreement in the first place. Nobody wants to hear a "giant sucking sound."

98. PROTECTIONISM

Let's say you're a U.S. company in the business of making baseball gloves. You make a pretty good glove, have a good brand, and good relationships with the stores that sell your gloves. You make a decent living at it, not a ton of money, but a decent living despite the fact that your business costs are on the upswing—higher labor costs, health care costs, energy prices, you name it.

Then, suddenly, a new Asian manufacturer hits the market with good gloves—not much of a brand, but a much lower price, because of lower labor costs, health care costs, and so forth. You want to compete, but you can't. So if you had good friends in high places, you might ask the federal government to impose a tariff on the import of baseball gloves. That's an example of protectionism.

What You Should Know

Protectionism is a deliberate economic policy implemented to guide or restrain trade between countries, mainly through protective tariffs, or taxes, on imported goods, but sometimes through import quotas or some other tactic. The goal may be to collect tax revenue, but is more likely to protect the fortunes of specific businesses or industries within the country imposing the protective measures.

Protectionism has led to numerous battles and debates through history. Recent policy has leaned away from protectionism as more economists and policymakers embrace the benefits of globalization. Protectionism has been looked on less favorably since the disastrous protectionist initiative during the Great Depression as part of the Smoot-Hawley Tariff Act of 1930. That act tried to support U.S. businesses by protecting them from imports, but all it did was hurt foreign economies, which then spent less on U.S. goods, prolonging the Depression. That experience is the cornerstone of most economists' feelings today: that protectionism ultimately hurts those it is trying to help, and prolongs the life of inefficient businesses and industries to the long-term detriment of everyone.

Protectionist sentiment and activity often leads to the slippery slope known as a *trade war*. Country A slaps a duty on a product from Country B, so Country B slaps a duty on a product from Country A. And so it goes, until trade between the two nations is all but choked off. Both sides have certain industries that gain from the protection and certain other industries that lose because their export markets are cut off. In the end, nobody wins.

Some argue that protectionism only levels the playing field; that is, foreign goods hitting U.S. shores aren't taxed, while domestic producers are. The argument gains strength when looking at many overseas businesses operating with overt or covert government subsidies. But still the prevailing opinion is that outright protectionism in most cases does more harm than good.

Why You Should Care

Why you should care about protectionism is really the flip side of why you should care about trade agreements and free trade. Protectionism might help you save a job, but you need to ask yourself whether you should be engaged in that activity anyway if there are lower-cost producers elsewhere. And protectionism is a two-way street—sure, your job can be protected. But suppose you work in an industry that exports to other countries, and they decide to enact trade barriers on the products you produce? You would lose on that one.

If you think it through, you should prefer natural competition and evolution of comparative advantage. Protectionism and especially trade wars can get really nasty. Even if you work for a protected industry, supporting such an idea may hurt you in the long run.

99. INTERNATIONAL MONETARY FUND (IMF) AND WORLD BANK

The International Monetary Fund and World Bank are household names for most who watch the evening news, yet most don't understand their roles in the world economy. And their roles are not without controversy on the world stage.

What You Should Know

The International Monetary Fund is kind of a United Nations of money and monetary policy. Originally created at the end of World War II, its purpose and goal was to stabilize exchange rates and create world policies for monetary exchange by influencing the macroeconomic policies of member countries. It conducts economic research, acts to advise and help member nations with financial policy, and has also assumed a role as lender of last resort in economic crises, mainly to the benefit of underdeveloped nations.

Originally chartered with forty-four countries, today's IMF has 188 countries, and with a few exceptions, maps the membership in the United Nations almost exactly. It is located in Washington, D.C. Funding and government are complicated, but not surprisingly the United States is both the largest provider of funds and also carries the greatest voting weight on decisions. Some countries bristle at the power of larger members (referred to as the "imperial power of the north" by the late Venezuelan president Hugo Chavez) but maintain membership because it is a condition to be able to borrow funds on the world stage.

The IMF has met some criticism over the years for funding "military dictatorships," and more recently for suggesting dubious economic policy, which got Argentina in trouble in 2001. Many of its critics consider its policies and recommendations to be overly rooted in Keynesian policies of taxation and government intervention, not the more recently stylish monetary policies (see #57 and #56). Still, over the years, IMF activities have done a lot to stabilize international economics, foster globalization, and help countries make informed economic decisions.

The World Bank is also located in Washington, D.C., and was born of the same conference at the end of WWII that created the IMF. But it is less involved in economic policy and monetary exchange and rather more involved in actually funding development of infrastructure and socioeconomic programs in underdeveloped countries. A stated purpose is the creation of an environment suitable for "investment, jobs, and sustainable growth." The World Bank faces some of the same criticisms as the IMF for trying to impose a U.S.- or Western-centric approach onto recipient nations, which often doesn't work, or worse, *criticism* creates conflict within and among these nations. The World Bank obtains funds by selling bonds and from contributions from about forty of its 187 member countries.

Why You Should Care

The activities of the IMF and World Bank aren't likely to affect your daily life. It's nice to know that there are organizations in place to serve to develop international cohesion and progress on a world front, and to coordinate globalization, at least to a degree.

100. WORLD TRADE ORGANIZATION

While the IMF and the World Bank concern themselves with matters of international finance, the World Trade Organization (WTO) concerns itself with the process, policies, and procedures of international trade. The WTO as known today is relatively new, dating back to 1995, succeeding the General Agreement on Tariffs and Trade, or GATT, formed in 1947.

What You Should Know

The World Trade Organization regulates trade and the process of trade between participating countries, providing a procedure and framework for developing trade policies and agreements. The goal is to promote free trade, fair trade, and to stimulate economic growth through trade.

The WTO and its predecessors provided an active forum to negotiate and discuss trade policy. Every few years a new "round" of discussions occurs, typically resulting in the relaxation or elimination of tariffs on certain goods, like agricultural commodities, and new rules, like the antidumping rules adopted in the 1960s. (Antidumping makes it illegal for nations to "dump" goods on another country's market at prices below cost or below prices charged in the home market.) The recent "Uruguay Round" commenced in 1986 and was the largest to date, lasting eighty-seven months, including 123 countries, creating the WTO as an organizational framework, and creating new rules around intellectual property, among other accomplishments. The "Doha Round," which has been in progress since 2001, is expanding beyond traditional trade issues to cover environmental concerns, and is aimed at the needs of developing countries. It has been bogged down by concerns, mainly about agricultural trade and farm subsidies.

The WTO and its negotiations do not actually produce tariffs or other trade policies; they instead create a forum or framework of fairness for doing so. WTO members cannot discriminate against other WTO members; that is, the same trade policies and tariffs apply to any country selling a similar good, and member countries agree to treat each other as "most favored nations." WTO rules also call for transparency and clarity on tariffs and tariff schedules.

The WTO has gone a long way toward fostering globalization; without the WTO world trade would likely be much more tangled up with complex, "one-off" policies and high tariffs. Critics of the WTO make the same arguments as critics of globalization—that it makes it harder to protect local industries, and causes greater income divergence between rich and poor nations. Agreements can take a long time, and some complain that traditional industries like local agriculture can be hurt by WTO actions and agreements.

Why You Should Care
The WTO and resulting globalization play an important role in expanding trade and making more goods available to more

people worldwide at more reasonable prices. The trade wars that would result without WTO would make the supply of some products and commodities unpredictable and expensive. The WTO groundwork creates stability in international trade, so you can take comfort in finding what you buy today at similar prices tomorrow.

101. G8 ECONOMIC SUMMITS

You hear a lot about the "G" summits on the nightly news and from various other news sources. But what exactly are these summits? Are they just suit-and-tie photo-ops for the participating nations and leaders, or do they really accomplish something? And most of all, how do they affect you?

What You Should Know

The G8, or Group of Eight, sessions were started in 1975 for the economic heavyweights of the Northern Hemisphere in response to the global energy crisis of 1974. Originally, it was the G6—the United States, France, Germany, Italy, Japan, and the United Kingdom—but in recent years it expanded to include Canada and then Russia. These eight countries represent 14 percent of the world's population but some 60 percent of the world's economic activity.

The summits include the heads of government—presidents, vice presidents, and prime ministers—as well as finance ministers and special envoys. They are informal in nature, with no specified outcome and little in the way of administrative structure. Topics are broad and include most anything of global concern, including economic development, world health, energy, environment, trade, terrorism and political turmoil, and an assortment of other issues that not only concern the eight nations but also the world at large. Leaders may discuss and come to an agreement on an approach to an issue, but these agreements aren't binding, and action is subject to subsequent actions on the part of participating country governments, the United Nations, the World Bank, and other organizations.

The G8 has famously provided the setting for sizeable and visible protests, recently on issues related to the environment and globalization (see #91), and has also been linked to acts of terrorism, as in 2005 when the London bus bombings occurred while a G8 summit was being held in Scotland.

Why You Should Care

The G8 summits are so high-level and far-reaching that little of what comes out of them will affect you directly or immediately. But it's good to keep track of world direction on key issues such as the three Es—economy, environment, and energy—that are discussed at these summits, and will affect all of us eventually. Aside from specific outcomes, these summits will give you a sense of what the current global priorities are.

INDEX

tranche – slice, section, portion